ELLA MARIE HOLMES

Sowing Seed in Assam

MISSIONARY LIFE AND LABOURS
IN NORTHEAST INDIA

By
E. MARIE HOLMES
of the
American Baptist Foreign Mission Society

Introduction by
HELEN BARRETT MONTGOMERY

ILLUSTRATED

NEW YORK   CHICAGO
Fleming H. Revell Company
LONDON   AND   EDINBURGH

Printed in the United States of America

New York: 158 Fifth Avenue
Chicago: 17 North Wabash Ave.
London: 21 Paternoster Square
Edinburgh: 75 Princes Street

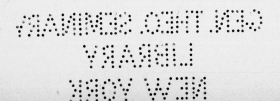

INTRODUCTION

AMONG all the missionaries whom the Woman's American Baptist Foreign Mission Society has sent into the field, one of the most individual and useful was Miss E. Marie Holmes of Gauhati, Assam. Miss Holmes was sent to take care of a newly-established Girls' School in Gauhati, and of this she made a unique institution, known throughout the length and breadth of Assam.

The education of women is still in a very backward state in that part of the world, and in deciding the curriculum and plans for her new school, Miss Holmes felt that there was great danger of taking the girls away from the simple surroundings in which they must live. She put no great amount of money in pretentious buildings, therefore, but used the cottage-plan and followed the native line of architecture in the very primitive buildings which she erected. Each of these buildings housed a family of girls of different ages, with a housemother. The girls were taught native cooking and sewing. Weaving looms were set up on the veranda, and all the arts of everyday life in their own villages were taught. Little waif-children and babies were taken in, and the house-family of girls were taught to take care of these little ones. Lessons in baby-nurture which were none the less loving, because thoroughly scientific, were given the girls. They learned how to bathe and clothe and feed the children.

At once a change of feeling in regard to the education of girls began to be evident in the community. It had been felt before that girls who were sent to the Christian school became too highly educated and too refined for ordinary life, and were of no use to their families. Whether this criticism were just or not, it could no longer be made concerning the Gauhati girls, who were educated not away from, but into their surroundings. The school soon came to the attention of the Government, and has had a constant and flattering growth ever since.

Perhaps Miss Holmes was distinguished even more as an evangelist than as a teacher. Certainly the deep passion of her heart was to get so near to the people that she could share their lives and troubles, and lead them sympathetically to the great Burden-Bearer.

After some years Miss Holmes was obliged to return home to care for a beloved sister who had gone out to assist her in the kindergarten department, and became a victim of tuberculosis. She stayed at home with her sister Nettie until the death of the latter in 1922. She then returned to Assam, intending to give herself wholly to evangelistic work; but found herself physically unable to endure the strain.

There is an unusual quality that runs through Miss Holmes' narrative. She makes you see things and hear things, almost as if you were on the ground, and her reactions are not ordinary ones. It is a great pleasure to be asked to write a brief Introduction to a book written by one who endeared herself, not only to her colleagues, but to the Board which sent her forth. I sincerely hope for it a great future of usefulness.

HELEN BARRETT MONTGOMERY

DEAR FATHER AND MOTHER-MINE:

While writing these pages, I have thought much of the debts I owe you and can never pay. Before I was born you began the second-mile service of love that has not once lagged in all these years. You never bargained for wages and have taken no account of hours, though working overtime; have never gone on strike nor taken holiday.

For all the clothes you have provided, laundered, and mended, for all the sweeping and dusting, for all the cooking and nursing and comforting, for all the treats you provided through sacrifice, for happy playtime and evenings around the lamp, for bedtime kisses and prayers, for a refuge with ever-open door to warm love that understands without questioning, for my home and my sisters, for all precious memories of your love, I offer this little book in loving and grateful tribute.

Affectionately your grown-up Girl,

ELLA MARIE

Redlands, Calif.

Contents

ILLUSTRATIONS

I

"LULLABY DAYS"

THEY were willing to have me although they did not need me and could not afford me. Already there were little blue-eyed Bertha, four years and a month, and little brown-eyed Maude, who came as a present to Bertha the day two candles burned on her birthday cake. There was Mother's mother to care for, too. There was house rent to pay and Father's salary of fifty dollars a month was the only income.

When two candles burned on my birthday cake, Mother's fourth baby had been heir to the baby carriage for a month, and I had been promoted to the crib. Nettie, this fourth baby, was the most indispensable member of the family. I have tried to picture the years without her, in her stead an additional dress or two every year for the rest of us, an occasional extra dish on the table, and slightly different tasks filling Mother's days. Had my parents given me life then decided that they could not afford to add to their family and had denied life to my younger sister, they would have robbed me of the greatest enrichment my life has known; they would have denied to my other sis-

11

ters and to themselves the benison of that quiet
life whose daily living through the years taught
us all the strength and beauty of goodness.
Scores of men and women, and hosts of little children, would have found life poorer and more difficult had Nettie not come their way. The members of our little family group were as different
from one another as though they were unrelated,
yet each brought a peculiar contribution that
seemed essential to the best development of the
others. In spite of our faults and differences,
clannish love and loyalty welded us together in
happy home-life—that seal of God's presence
among men.

One of my earliest memories is of Mother putting us to bed at night. After she had heard our
prayers, tucked us in and kissed us good-night,
she would stoop to turn down the wick of the little
flat-bottomed oil lamp on the tiny platform landing at the top of the stairs, her white, starched
apron gleaming in the lamp-light. "No, no.
That's too low; higher than that," we would call
out until the flame was adjusted to suit us.
Leaving her little ones safely tucked-in for the
night, their happy whispers and giggles doing
short but hopeless battle with weariness and
sleep, Mother would go down the narrow, un-
carpeted stairs to a heaped up mending basket,
one ear open for sounds of the children up stairs
and the other open to whatever Father might have

to recount of the day's doings as he puffed at his
pipe and turned the pages of his paper before his
preliminary sleep on the dining-room lounge. Not
the pay envelopes, but those evening hours was
the "day's reward" for Father and Mother all
those hard-working years of our childhood.

After Mother had lowered the lamp and left us,
Bertha would tell fairy tales or Mother Goose
rhymes, punctuating the tales with yawns as her
voice sounded more and more remote until there
was no listening ear to hear what befell the prince
in the enchanted castle.

There is another childhood memory that I thank
God American children need no longer have.
Often we ran errands for neighbours. I was six,
possibly seven, years old when a neighbour sent me
to buy a bucket of beer; "rushing the growler"
was the very descriptive phrase used to describe
the process. It was midsummer. The saloon was
four or five blocks away, down by the Seventh-
street wharf. A short cut led through several
lumber-yards with cinder driveways. I took the
short cut, lifting my bare feet gingerly over the
rough cinders, hot under the midday sun. When
I rang the bell at the side door marked "Ladies'
Entrance" a white-aproned bartender opened
the door, lifted me and the bucket in his arms,
and taking me into the saloon, stood me on the
counter where I was made much of while he filled
the can with frothy beer. I went home with a

fistful of large salty pretzels in one hand, and in
the other the can of beer for which service my
neighbour gave me two cents.

The only pennies we had, were earned doing
errands for neighbours. In those days a penny
would buy a pickle with a piece of brown paper
at the end to catch the dripping vinegar, a strip of
fresh cocoanut fished by the grocer from a jar of
water (it may have been cocoanut milk that was
in the jar). You could get two long black licorice
shoestrings for a penny, or gamble on chocolate
turtles, some of which hid a penny within their
cream-centers, or have a grab-bag of left-over can-
dies with sometimes a surprise ring or trinket in
it. But you could not buy less than two cents
worth of beefsteak candy. Beefsteak candy was
a kind of fondant with white streaks through it for
the fat, and pink folds for the lean meat.

Father and Mother did not attend church in
those days but they sent us children to Sunday
school. In the afternoons we attended a mission
school where we were given little wooden barrels
to fill with money and return. I got enough pennies in my barrel to make a pleasant jingle when I
shook it. Once when I happened to shake the
barrel with the slit side down, a penny rolled out.
More shaking brought forth a second penny. Two
pennies in my hand at once! That had not happened before since I knew about beefsteak candy.
If both of those pennies were mine I could sample

beefsteak candy. Some day I would have two pennies at once. I would save my next penny until I got another and then I could buy the candy. As I started to drop the pennies back through the slit in the barrel it occurred to me that it was useless to wait to save the pennies when I might just as well borrow the two right in my hand and pay them back when I had earned two cents. So I ate two cents worth of beefsteak candy and it was so good! Better even than I had thought it would be. For some days after I did not get a penny for errands, but I went around to the candy store and looked at the beefsteak. There was not very much left and maybe the next lot would not be so good.

So I went home and got the barrel just to see if I could tell how many pennies were in it. After I had shaken out two, I visited the candy store again and had more than a look at the candy. After several other beefsteak feasts, there was nothing left in the barrel to jingle when I shook it.

Although pennies were scarce when we were children, and we knew but little of confectioners' goodies, still we had frequent family treats. How Mamma ever managed it, on her ten and twelve dollars a week, has ever been to me a mystery. Every Sunday there was a tin plate of brittle taffy that broke in kaleidoscope figures when hit on the bottom of the cooling pan with a knife handle. Sometimes there was a cake with icing or custard between the layers; or there was popped corn, pudding which had been frozen in the snow or frost; there were black walnuts or hickory nuts, cracked between two flat irons and the kernels extracted with wire hairpins.

There were eventful days with a swing in the woodshed on which we took turns. A " go " lasted until the swing came still after hard pushing while we recited:

> *" Charlie Buck had money enough*
> *To lock it up in the storehouse;*
> *But when he died he closed his eyes*
> *And never saw money any more.*
> *A high swing, a low swing,*
> *A very good swing for Charlie Buck."*

A board over a keg or a box see-sawed to the tune of:

> *" See-saw, Margery Daw,*
> *Johnnie shall have a new master;*
> *He shall make but a penny a day*
> *Because he can't work any faster."*

Button-strings were all the rage in those days and every youngster teased her mother for pretty buttons. When a string of threaded beauties was swung awhirl by an expert then held taut at either end while the buttons spun elliptical circles of glistening beauty, the sight made all envious beholders hold their breath with admiration. An exchange of buttons was made with all the haggling

of an Oriental bazaar or a Los Angeles real estate
agent.

Annually, with summer clothes appeared " light
boxes." These were generally shoe-boxes with
stars, moons, fruit, flower and animal shapes cut
from the pasteboard and the spaces filled in with
brightly coloured tissue paper, a candle within the
box making the gay paper cuts shine brightly on
dark nights. A string pulled through one end of
the box enabled it to be dragged over the pavement
behind the happy owner. Some boxes were built
two or three tiers high. It was a dangerous toy for
little children and fatal accidents probably brought
it into disfavour.

Ring-games were part of summer sport, too.
While fathers and mothers sat on front porches
enjoying the cool and rest after the long day of
hard work, and called back and forth from porch to
porch in neighbourly fashion, their children made
the night merry with " Lazy Mary," " The Farmer
in the Dell," " Waiting for a Partner," " Go In
and Out the Windows," " London Bridge," " Here
We Go Round the Mulberry Bush," " Drop the
Handkerchief," and other childish roundelays.

During the winter different cliques used to get
up shows to which an admission of from two to
ten pins was charged. The show would sometimes
be a trick, a story acted out by the children dressed
up for their parts, or by paper people on a paper
stage; sometimes it would be a real program with

pieces, songs, dances, and dogs and cats doing tricks.

All the year around Saturday was bath-night, and that was such a good time when we lived in a house with a zinc tub with a slippery, sloping head. We would soap the slide, sit up at the top and speed down into the bath with a splash. A bath in a wooden tub on the kitchen floor was not nearly so popular.

When, for some weeks, great earthen pipes were strung along one side of a street at the back of our house, there was endless fun playing tunnel and crawling through the pipes a whole block's length. Then one sad day the pipes were lowered into the ditch, and after the workmen went home we played tunnel one more last time before the dirt was thrown over the pipes. When I emerged from the far end of the tunnel, hands, face, white apron, stockings, shoes, were daubed with red clay. I did not dare let my mother see me like that and did not know how to keep her *from* seeing me. One of the boys suggested that I get under the old wooden pump which stood in front of the candy store and have one of the children pump while the others scrubbed me. This promised some improvement at least, so I scraped away at the clay while we stole along the back alley to the pump. I stooped under the spout and was pumped upon and scrubbed with a vengeance, but came forth from the operation feeling and looking worse than before. Running, weeping and wailing, I sped in search of the mother I had before sought to escape, while little rivulets irrigated all the block-and-a-half which lay between the pump and home.

On one occasion I tumbled accidently into one of the nicest times I ever had. Mother used to sit backwards on the window-sill to wash windows. One day I sat thus in a second-story window to see what it felt like. I turned a somersault backwards into a trash-barrel where a broken thin red glass pitcher stuck into my foot. When mother picked me up she held me close and had everybody jumping around filling the orders she gave. After the glass was extracted I was put to bed in Nettie's cot in Mother's room and I had to stay there day and night for some time. But I enjoyed it immensely. All the children wanted to give me some of their treasures; Mother used to sit by me and feed me; and every evening Father brought me home a roll-picture advertising the Atlantic and Pacific Tea Stores, a brand of soap or condensed milk, or an insurance company. Sweet to my soul was the sight of the anxious faces of my sisters and little friends as they asked how I felt. As I got better and these same children presumed upon old familiarity I gave them to understand that a girl with a cut foot could never again be just the same ordinary child she had been before.

After my foot had healed, my mother made me, out of my grandmother's old circular cape, the

most beautiful black satin dress with a guimpe of
yellow silk and a spray of buttercups embroidered
around the yoke. I must have looked well in it,
for Mother told Father to take me by Uncle Jim's.
Now Uncle Jim kept a store and Mother's object
in sending me to him was to make him envious of
his poorer brother's treasures. It was Sunday
afternoon but he took us down stairs and gave me
a bag of round dome-shaped cakes with pink and
chocolate icing on them. That same afternoon on
our way home Father took me into a power-house
with great throbbing engines and whirling wheels;
then to a fire-house where one of the firemen held
me up so that I could rub the soft velvet noses of
the big horses. When I got back home with my
bag of cakes and stories of adventure I found it
just as interesting to be well and have a black satin
dress with buttercups on it and be carried around
and shown off as it had been to have a cut foot and
sympathetic folk hovering around. There was
some sort of pleasure in everything that happened.

II

SCHOOL AND FACTORY YEARS

WHEN I was about eight years old Father went to be a clerk in his brother's store about seven miles from Washington; so for four years we had a taste of country life. If I had to choose between the two, I would rather give my small children four years of country life than give them four years of college later on. Impulses and influences took root in those four years that have been as sheltering vines, as flowering plants, and as fruitful trees, in the years that have followed. Days there were out-of-doors, walks through fields bespangled with daisies and buttercups, through woods fragrant with arbutus hiding Spring's loveliness under Winter's dead leaves, while mating birds sang love-songs as they built nests and brooded their eggs. The nights were cozy, with the family circle gathered around a lamp on the table and pets sleeping at our feet. So far as income was concerned we had no more money than we had possessed when in the city, but we had all the wealth of out-of-doors, so we did not feel poor.

Not only does the family circle seem closer and cozier in a country home, but in a rural community the spirit of neighbourliness seems warmer and stronger than it is possible for community feeling to be in a town or city where neighbours know little of one another and have many diverse interests away from home and neighbourhood. Much has been written of the narrowness of country life and of the gossiping propensities of country folk, so that these two terms pass unchallenged. "Narrowness," where by day the eye follows long stretches of road through green fields and by rugged streams until lost amongst hills and great trees that stretch their finger tips to touch heaven's blue! A sweep of the eye from those upstretched trees, draws a great circle joining heaven and earth at its circumference, while all the land is aquiver with living, growing plants nodding and bowing in friendliness while busy creatures work in their shade or wing their way joyously to heights beyond reach of the tallest tree. By night the darkness, undimmed by glaring artificial lights, draws the gaze above where God's glory blazes in stars unveiled by smoke. Change the green of summer to the rioting colours of autumn or the quiet, glistening white of winter and you have new characters, new costumes, on the same matchless stage stirring the soul and whetting the mind until they are restless as with growing-pains.

In the dozen or score of houses nestling under trees, by brooks or on hilltops, live men, women and children whose lives are rich in every great human experience. Here babies come, "trailing clouds of glory" that all are unconsciously conscious of; they grow into childhood with its play and school, into manhood and maidenhood with its beauty, work and love. Marriage-bells ring and new homes are built; sickness and sorrow come with their chastening power; tragedy creeps in and death enters its claim. In a country community these things are not material for newspaper reports; they do not occur daily, and so make little impress. But through the years they happen to flesh-and-blood people whose Christian names are spoken in every household, whose traits, ambitions, abilities, failures, successes, are fairly estimated by their neighbours. The "gossip" of the countryside is usually natural curiosity sympathetically busy, not with strangers or acquaintances, but with friends and well-known neighbours. But out of this so-called "narrowness" and gossip have come poets to sing songs of nature, home, and love, with such constraining sweetness that all the world sings with them; and from country homes have come pioneer souls of vision and daring to lighten dark continents and to open doors of freedom for those carried from thence into slavery.

A year ago Mother, Bertha and I drove out to Landover and walked over the old landmarks. We went to the little brown house below the station where Mother had sought to augment her income

by boarding four of the men working on the Chesa-
peake Railroad, and receiving for her labour worth-
less stock in the liquidated company—scrip for two
hundred dollars that would not reduce her grocery
bill by a dollar. A brook running alongside the
road in front of the brown house, bound Miss Joe's
apple orchard where grew the most wonderful rus-
set apples that ever gave a child pain in the
stomach. Mother did not whip her children often,
but once, when she wanted to administer needed
chastisement to me, I ran around the big flower
bed in the side yard. As my fleet little mother
was gaining upon me, I scampered down the ter-
race, across the road, right in and through the
" branch " where my mother halted while I sought
the refuge of Miss Joe's friendly tree and the comfort of her apples. At dusk I went sheepishly
home and was sent to bed. I was wretchedly unhappy and ashamed of my naughtiness, but could
not frame a confession with my tongue. So I scrib-
bled a note which ran: " Dear Mamma, I love you
and am sorry I am so bad." The crumpled paper
was hid under my pillow until Mother came upstairs to fix me for the night, when I tied it to one
of her apron strings.

There was no Protestant church or Sunday
school in Landover when we first moved there.
Some of the mothers decided to build a Union
church. While the church was building the Sunday school, preaching services and prayer meeting

were held in our home. Here the preachers were
often entertained Tuesday and Sunday evenings,
and here, too, the ladies gave a dance and supper
for the benefit of the new church building. On
this occasion so many city-folk stayed all night
that we slept in beds crosswise, with chairs pulled
up to support the feet of the taller girls.

Because Mother did not approve of the teacher,
I was out of school for a year and a half in Landover. I then spent a year in Philadelphia where
I attended school. We moved to Baltimore shortly
after I returned from Philadelphia. I entered the
Baltimore schools about Easter and was placed in
the seventh grade. The Baltimore children had
been studying algebra all the year; I had never
heard of it. I had no patience with it. I found X
particularly exasperating and elusive. It was never
the same thing twice in succession. Other children got five and ten home-problems correct every
night while I had not the faintest idea as to how
to proceed. Ah, Emma Lou! I can sympathize
with you. But I retrieved myself on the Easter
composition that we had to write in school. My
teacher and the principal gave me a private audience after school and bestowed high praise upon
my composition, then declared that the child who
wrote that paper could easily master algebra—as
though bursting bulbs and butterflies with newly
acquired wings had anything in common with life-
less X! Papa could not get work as easily as

we had supposed he could, so after about two weeks at school I ceased to bother about X and accompanied Bertha and Maude to the factory where Bertha was bookkeeper and Maude operated a machine.

We left home in mornings about twenty or twenty-five minutes after six and by steady walking arrived at the factory just as the whistles blew seven. It was a large overall and shirt factory about half a block deep. We walked upstairs to the third or fourth floor. There were windows at front and back, but the centre of the room was quite dark except for lighted gas jets. A great engine at the back of the room revolved rods which ran under long tables and operated machines at which women bent. The operators worked piecework. As one hand pulled the garment from the machine and dropped it on the floor to the right, the other hand automatically reached for another garment from the pile stacked on a box at the left of the machine.

I was floor-girl. Going up and down the aisles I picked up the overalls, folded and piled them on a table until I had a stack that reached from my shoulder to the top of my head. Around this I stretched my little arms and carried the burden to the great table at the front of the room where the work was examined. There was no time to sit or rest until the noon whistle blew. Then from paper bags we brought out our sandwiches, fruit and cake. Some girls brought bottles of tea or coffee which they poured into tin cups with handles bound with cloth so they could be held over the gas jets, to heat their contents. From twelve to twelve-thirty the clock travelled at a pace designed to make up for the lagging of time before and after that period. Hardly were the contents of the paper sacks disposed of when the twelve-thirty whistles blew, the deafening din of machinery restarted, and work commenced again. I continued plodding the same round until five-thirty when there was a rush for four faucets at the sink where about a hundred girls sought to wash off the blue dye and change into dresses fit to wear on the street. My knees shook with exhaustion as I walked downstairs and joined the jostling crowds on the sidewalks,—all homeward bound.

When we came to the corner, dismayed to see Bertha cross the cartracks rather than join the waiting crowds, I cried out to her, " Oh, Bertha! Aren't we going to ride home? I'm so tired!" Still walking briskly, Bertha answered, " I'm afraid not, honey; we can't afford it. You won't feel so tired when we have been out in the air awhile, and have gotten away from the crowds."

I wanted to sit on the curb and cry. I thought I never could walk home. How gladly at that moment I would have gone back to school and that algebraic X. Let X be the number of blocks home. At every crossing I counted them to keep the tears back and my legs moving. Carfare for the three of us would have been fifteen cents, three-fifths of my ten-hour-day's earnings.

The next day the program was the same and for many days thereafter. On Saturday I received my week's wages, a dollar-and-a-half, that is, twenty-five cents a day, two-and-a-half cents an hour. After a few months I was promoted to a cording machine and ran cords in the fronts of men's shirts. On this work (by taking all of my mistakes home to make right at night) I made as much as two dollars and forty cents in one week. Then I went to another factory to operate a button machine for two dollars a week. Here I broke the record by sewing on (as I remember it) 2,000 buttons a day! Occasionally rush orders necessitated our working overtime—sometimes until eight or nine o'clock at night. At such times the piece-workers were paid for the work done and time-workers received as compensation for the extra two or three hours' work a box of half a dozen fried oysters with a piece of pickle and some crackers. This in the the years 1896-1899 in the city of Baltimore!

Organized labour has made some mistakes in policy and control, but it is owing to its efforts that a labourer usually receives something like a worthy recompense for hire and a child of twelve does not have to work in factories. Had labour not organized, the conditions of 1896 would probably still be maintained; employers would be living in even more palatial homes and labourers be living in the wretched abodes that to this day stand in mute accusation along the railroad tracks in the mining sections of West Virginia, marring the beauty of the fair hills of that state.

One morning on my way to work, I saw a large billboard announcing that Maude Adams was playing at a local theater. Now the previous week I had read many beautiful things concerning Miss Adams' private life and professional career. As a little girl of five or six, I had sat with Bertha and one of her girl-friends in the peanut gallery to see "A Farmer's Daughter," and when I was but twelve, a neighbour in Philadelphia had taken me to see "Faust." Dozens of times since that day I had acted some of those scenes out before admiring youngsters. An old longing to make vast audiences laugh and cry at my will, was revived with all the vitality of hibernated hope. I could not afford the price of a ticket to see Maude Adams, so I wrote the celebrity a letter telling her that I was undecided whether to be a writer or an actress, that my people did not want me to go on the stage but that I thought I would do it anyway, only I did not know how to go about it, so was hoping that she would send me instructions for which I enclosed a stamp. This was the method followed to secure instructions concerning anything that was advertised in a *Fireside Companion* that used to come to our house in Landover.

All that week Bertha and Maude walked home
far too slowly to suit me, so eager was I for Maude
Adams' letter that I confidently expected each
night. But the answer never came and my two
postage stamps and the paper and envelope that I
had bought at a notion store, were wasted. But
my desire did not die easily. I watched the want
ads, and the summer that I was fifteen I saw that
two sixteen-year-old girls were wanted to help out
in a cast. They were to apply at a certain ter-
race. I thought that I knew where this was and
set out for it in high glee, mentally reading newspaper accounts of Ella Marie Holmes' beautiful
home life, her deeds of charity, and the splendour
of her professional career. I clipped some of the
most glowing recitals to send to Maude Adams
without an enclosed stamp. I hunted for that ter-
race until dark, but found it not and then went sor-
rowfully home.

While working in factories I never went out in
the evening. If there were no work to rip I used
to read my sister Nettie's books from the Enoch
Pratt Library. After Father got work and our
finances were more promising, I had another year
at school. One Friday afternoon my teacher read
aloud from *Hiawatha*. It was hard to keep the
tears back, I was so happy. It reminded me of
the song of the brook at Landover and of the
passing of the breeze in the tree-tops in the wood
where arbutus grows. All sense of words and all

trend of a tale were lost in the flow of words and their music. This was a new thing to share with Nettie.

It was about this time that I became interested in atheism. My father and his five brothers had been brought up according to the strictest sect of Scotch Presbyterianism. On weekdays they were driven to school in a carriage, but on Sunday they had to walk to church and Sunday school. They were not allowed to whistle or sing. The Bible and Sunday-school paper were the only legitimate Sabbath literature. I judge that the father's skilfully hidden love found expression in rules of conduct and economy of expenditure. The mother was loving and generous as she dared to be. The boys grew up with nothing but bitterness for their father's religion, and four of them lived to good old age and were buried without giving recognition at all during their later years to religion. When I was a girl my father was still an atheist and I was trying to be one, too.

From the library I got Robert Ingersoll's works and kindred books and read them. I also read much of the Hebrews and thought they must have known much more about the Christ they rejected, than the Gentiles who accepted Him could possibly know.

My sister Nettie was my only close friend, and I did not share my doubts and rebellion with her. For to my little sister, faith in God as always present, always wise and loving in His guidance, gifts and denials, was as natural and as sustaining as nursing is to a babe. I hope not many children of fifteen are doomed to silent waging of battles as desperate as I fought when at that age. I took nothing for granted, accepted nothing on faith, challenged everything, doubted everything and questioned everything, from immortality to the presence of sin, sorrow and weariness. And all this mental warfare was silently waged with no one to know or help. I was wretchedly unhappy and longed to go alone to some woods where, with no one to see or know, I might seek God if haply I might find Him.

Mother compelled me to attend afternoon Sunday school with my sisters. My teacher was a good, kind woman, but she was not on very familiar terms with God. She read us what was written in her quarterly for she had nothing better written in her head and heart. I promised one of the girls with whom I worked, to visit her Sunday school one morning and here I found a teacher who was different. She possessed a quality that the other teacher lacked. She and God were good friends; she stayed close by Him so that He could send her on errands. I think that she had known sorrow and had wrested sweetness and sympathy from it. Some of my questions she answered without my having to ask them.

For a month or more that inward battle went

on with renewed fury, but still no outward sign.
My new Sunday-school teacher asked me to attend
an evening evangelistic service at her church. I
went alone. A white-haired saint stood in front
of a vast concourse of us and spoke of God our
Father, and of our Brother, Christ the Saviour.
The light on the old man's face, the earnestness of
his speech, his confidence in God and his yearning
love for his fellows, made his simple message
eloquent. After the benediction I stole out and
walked home along the wide, parked street of
Eutaw Place. Away from the church the streets
were deserted. There was no moon. The stars
were close and friendly. To them I lifted my face
and voice: "Oh, God!" I cried, "I don't know
who you are or what you are; I don't know where
you are nor how to come to you, but I need you.
I'm making a bungle of things and I'm so unhappy.
Take charge of me, dear God." The stars and I
have been in league ever since that night. Quietly
I finished my walk home. As a wee child losing
sight of its mother in a crowd, runs hither and yon,
becoming ever more terrified and fearful, then
catching sight of the familiar face, finds shelter in
protecting arms and after one or two gulping
breaths, nestles a tear-stained face in the haven of
mother's breast—thus that night was I comforted
by God.

In the dark and quiet of my room I definitely
committed my way to Him, and as I review the

twenty-four years that have since passed, I find that all the days of all the years testify marvelously to His direction of my paths. Not yet do I understand the reason for some of the detours, the hard, rugged climbing, the foggy stretches, the lonely ways. But all that I *do* understand proves irresistibly and conclusively that the journey was wisely planned, is being personally conducted and leads to a desirable end. And so I do not find it difficult to trust, concerning those stretches that have been and are as yet obscure.

The next morning I got up a little earlier, copied a Bible verse on a slip of paper and memorized it on my way to work.   But I told no one of my experience, for a fortnight. Then I asked for baptism in my own church, and after doing this went home and told the folk that I had been converted. An aunt who was living with us, laughingly warned me that my hair was still red. The next morning we began saying grace before meals.

III

GETTING READY

AFTER joining the Church I was given a piece to recite on Children's Day. It was about millions in China dying unsaved. I thought it was sad and tried to make it appear so to others, but I had no idea whether these millions were dying unsaved from fire, pestilence, or sword. Never, to my knowledge, had I heard of missions, either home or foreign.

Shortly after my sixteenth birthday we moved back to Washington, where, for two years, I worked in a cousin's store. Later I cashiered in a grocery store and clerked in a drug store, doubling my salary and leisure and finding time to read. One Sunday when I was eighteen, Dr. Willingham of Richmond preached the first foreign mission sermon I ever heard. Immediately I decided to become a foreign missionary and was puzzled to know why all the young people who had heard the address had not made similar decisions. Again I was ignorant as to how to enter upon my chosen career. Miss Appler, my Sunday-school teacher at that time, gave me the address of our foreign mission society in Boston. I wrote them, expecting that in two weeks or so, I would be on my way to Africa. The letter from Boston stated that I

must have the equivalent of a High School education and some special training in addition, and that
twenty-five was the minimum age for entering foreign mission service. This time Ignorance stood
by Youth barring the gate to Paradise. A High
School education! And I had been in school but
five-and-a-half years all told! It would take me
until I was twenty-five to do what was required for
preparation.

I began at once by getting books from the library
and by reading Nettie's school books. And I
began to save. I wore blue gingham shirt-waists
—even on Sunday. I walked to and from work,
except when on night duty. In summer, when I
hankered for an ice-cream soda, I would walk up
to a drug-store window, stop a few minutes to look
at the soaps, perfumes, brushes, etc., displayed
there, then walk away wiping my lips and making
believe that I had been inside and had a soda.
The home-folk, laughing indulgently, remarked that
this was a new kind of fever and would probably
spend its course just as the stage-fever had done.
Handed-on clothes had always helped out with my
wardrobe, so most of my spending money changed
hands over second-hand bookstalls. When I heard
my first missionary sermon, I was the proud and
devoted possessor of about seventy-five books. I
supposed that when I should sail away as a missionary, I could take only such possessions as
might be carried in a suitcase or trunk, and so

thought there would be no room for books. In proof of the earnestness of my intentions, I distributed my books amongst my friends, keeping for myself only Watson's *Life of The Master*. This violent burning of bridges convinced the family that the new fever was a serious attack.

A friend told me about Northfield Seminary and I learned that I could earn a one-term scholarship by securing one hundred subscriptions to *The Record of Christian Work*. I straightway proceeded to do this. While canvassing for subscriptions I learned lessons that are on no school curriculum—lessons in human nature. Greater than the surprise of learning how little many people of comfortable circumstances feel that they can afford, apart from personal and household adornment, was my surprise to find how ready the poor often are to make an expenditure calculated to help some one else. Possibly they have formed the habit of doing without things; certainly they have learned the joy of sharing what one has. One of my most generous friends was my Sunday-school teacher. She herself had wanted to be a foreign missionary but her health prevented. After spending the trying summer days in an office, she devoted four nights a week through the hot summer months and her rare teaching ability to helping me with my books. Because of this loving service I was able to pass off most of my preparatory work when I entered Northfield Seminary, September, 1905.

The following four years at Northfield gave me much more than gleanings from books. There I had my first view of mountains, and needed no other testimony that the blood which nourished me had once coursed through the veins of men and women who stopped at their work to lift up their eyes unto the hills with all a highlander's love of lofty places. On the first Sunday afternoon at Northfield one of the teachers sat on the carpet of brown needles under the Cathedral Pines and read to us Dr. Van Dyke's story of " The Other Wise Man." Before the reading was over my arms had to shield a wet face buried in the needles. This was the first of many cherished experiences out of doors. There were tramps in snowstorms, long walks on frosty mornings when trees, bushes and houses glistened dazzlingly with jewelled icicles, when the ground was hid with sparkling gems; then hunts for the first arbutus and violets; Bird Day, when we tramped the hills, beautiful in fresh greens and spring blossoms and pungent with the smell of new life; Apple Blossom Sunday, when trees of pink posies quivered and bowed in the orchards, like little children in new spring dresses speaking pieces from a platform; Mountain Day, when frost had opened chestnut burrs and spilled the glossy brown nuts on the brilliant foliage with which the trees were having a quilting party against winter's cold. And there were close daily contacts with women of noble spirit, who shared with hundreds of eager girls the fine fruits of years of scholarship, culture and experience.

After the first semester my Sunday school paid a hundred dollars a year for my board and tuition. During the Christmas vacation I hired a hall in Washington and gave an evening of readings that usually netted sufficient to pay my carfare for the vacation and a surplus that took care of fees, books, clothes, etc. In my senior year expenses were heavy, but I came out a little ahead by giving readings in Massachusetts, Connecticut, Vermont, during the Easter recess, and by winning first prize in the Temperance prize-speaking contest.

Several times while at Northfield I was hard pressed for funds, but every need was wonderfully supplied, although I never spoke or wrote to anyone about my need of money. At noon one Monday in my Junior year, I was without a cent. That afternoon I had to pay a fifty-cent class fee and have a dollar and a quarter for a French book. Going to my room I found my room-mate out. Locking the door, I knelt by my bed, told God of my need and reminded Him that there was no one else to whom I could look for support. While I was still kneeling someone knocked at the door. It was the girl delivering the noon mail. She handed me a letter bearing the Washington postmark. Folded within a blank piece of paper was

a five-dollar bill. I do not know whom He used,
but I know that my Father sent me that money.
It had been mailed in Washington before I knew
that I would need it. " Before they call I will answer; and while they are yet speaking I will hear."
I needed only a dollar and seventy-five cents, but
received more than twice that amount. This is
God's " good measure, pressed down, and shaken
together, and running over." On another occasion
I had written my home letter but had no stamp
nor a cent with which to buy one. The same day
I had a letter from my sister Maude enclosing six
two-cent stamps, accompanied by a word saying
that she had them in her desk and thought that I
could use them.

"Childish, inconceivably childish!" you may say,
to suppose that the Creator and Sustainer of the
Universe Who stores forests of coal and rivers
of oil in the bowels of the earth, crowns Everest
with everlasting snow, and directs worlds in their
courses,—that this Creator and Sustainer takes
account of a little factory girl's need of a two-
cent postage stamp! Frankly I acknowledge
such personal care of the Creator for one of His
small creatures to be beyond the grasp of my
understanding, too, but it is in the realm of my
experience. And in my religion I am as ready to
be taught by forty years of life's experiences, as
in the study of a science I am open to laboratory
experiments and demonstrations to prove theories

of chemistry, physics, astronomy and botany, that as bare statements stagger my understanding.

Nor do these experiences of a personal God as a Father wisely, lovingly, intimately, active in all that conerns His children, rest only on my two-score years of experience: That is but a small rock in a mighty structure that has been millenniums in construction and on which shepherds, farmers, fishermen, housewives, generals, kings, poets and philosophers have wrought, testifying from the most varied experiences of their widely different stations in life, that God has dealt with them " as an eagle stirreth up her nest," fluttering over her young, spreading abroad her wings, taking them, bearing them on her wings; as a Shepherd feeding His flock in green pastures and by still waters, gathering the lambs in His arms, carrying them in His bosom and having thought for the mother sheep who find the way hard because of their con-cern for their young; as a Guide directing to the right hand and the left, arranging schedule, mak-ing record of the mileage, in mercy preventing, bringing safely to a desired haven and a good land; as a Lover loving with an everlasting love that many waters cannot quench, neither can the floods drown, drawing to Himself with bands of love, with love's insistence ever wooing to higher things; as a Father bearing His son in His mind and heart, taking him by his arm to teach him to take his first steps, correcting, instructing, pitying, afflicted in all His children's afflictions, running with royal welcome to greet a wayward son as he turns towards the Father's house; as a mother comforting a wounded spirit and bleeding heart. But even this array of word pictures did not suffice David, the shepherd-king-poet, the father of steadfast love for a rebellious son, as he reviewed God's care for him in all his chequered career; so faithful and rich in loving-kindness had he found God to be, that he said he would trust Him to take him up even in the inconceivable possibility of his father and mother forsaking him.

The coming of my friends prove that God counted their steps and mine and directed us to our meeting. Marvelously has their coming been timed and placed, bringing particular gifts to meet peculiar needs: a teacher when the mind needed direction, a physician when the body needed care, a strong arm when there was need to lift a load beyond my physical strength, a warm and understanding heart waiting at the end of every hard lonely passage, and most of the way there was my sister Nettie to cool my hot temper with her calm, to check my rash impulses with her sanity, to love me though knowing all my unloveliness, and to believe in me when for others I had no promise. These friends could no more have chanced to come in the fullness of time and at the appointed place of need, than Orion happens every year to wander across our winter skies; or than our American world-fliers chance to find new equipment and supplies waiting them at stated landing places. Since God has thought for the protection of a fern frond as He calls it from under the soil into the sunlight, I can believe that He is mindful of a factory girl's need of a two-cent stamp; since He times the stars along courses He has mapped out for them, is it impossible that our times are in His hands or that our steps are ordered by Him?

After graduating from Northfield I had a year at home in Washington attending normal school and substituting in the graded schools. This was of all years the one when I was most needed at home as my sister Maude was ill and my mother had persuaded her husband to let her come home to be nursed.

In September, 1910, I started in for a year's work at Newton Centre Theological Seminary. When I had been in the school but a month I was asked if I would accompany a bride and groom to Assam. I did not know where Assam was, but replied that I would go. There were but ten days in which to shop, dress-make and pack. I have always been glad that the time for preparation was so short, that there was no time to be dismal and no time for farewell parties.

My heart's desire was gratified when the steamship *Winifredian* pulled away from her dock in Boston, November 3, 1910. Just before the ap-

pointed hour for sailing we discovered that none
of my baggage was aboard! The transfer company had delivered it at the wrong dock. I wore a
coat-suit and had a nightbag with a "nightie,"
toothbrush and paste, soap-box and handkerchiefs.
Besides the bride and groom there were three other
passengers: an invalid who never left her cabin,
a dear Scotch spinster, and an interesting old
Irish lady whose morning and night refreshment
fumes escaped from her cabin to mine and were
different from the jube-jubes of which her breath
smelled when she came on deck. The invalid had
a beautiful fur-lined coat which she loaned me;
the Scotch lady contributed a blue, cotton blouse;
and the bride and groom graciously put their
steamer chairs close together so that one steamer
rug sufficed for them, in order to give me the use
of their second rug. Fog-horns were busy much
of the way, and we were nine days crossing. I
went to bed in the afternoons so that the stewardess could launder some things for me and dry
them in the engine-room. My trunk was located
and forwarded on a White Star liner and was waiting for me in Liverpool, when we arrived.

After the Scotch passenger had shown me Liver-
pool there was still a week before we sailed for
India. The bride and groom decided to remain in
Liverpool, so I went down to London by myself.
I arrived in the city after dark. I did not know
anyone in London and was so unfamiliar with Eng-

lish currency that twice I had to resort to offering
amazed clerks a palmful of miscellaneous coins
from which they culled the required cash. The
telephone directory showed no Y. W. C. A. hotel.
I called up the Association headquarters to en-
quire about accommodations and was told that
they made no provision for transients, but had a
home for working girls. Surely I belonged to that
class, but had difficulty in persuading the lady in
charge to admit me, since I was not seeking work
in London. The girls were going down to dinner
when I arrived. We passed in single file downstairs to the basement. In cafeteria style we
helped ourselves from stacks of heavy white plates
and cups and saucers. The cups were filled with
hot cocoa from a big white enamel pitcher, and two
steaming fat sausages and a boiled potato were put
on each of our plates as we passed to our places on
wooden benches running either side of two long
plank-tables. On round, wooden bread-boards
down the center of the table loaves of bread were
placed from which we cut slices as we wished them.

After dinner we went to our cubicles. A large
room with a narrow passage through the center
had the two sides partitioned into little narrow cur-
tained spaces furnished with a single cot, a wash-
stand and a little chair. After breakfast down in
the basement daily I sallied forth to the British Mu-
seum, the art galleries, the Tower, St. Paul's, and
Westminster Abbey, where Livingstone's floor-slab

stirred me as none of the monuments of the other departed great did. I experienced two thrills in the English metropolis. One was a real London fog, when all the shops were lighted at ten A. M. as at night, and the buses were as sparks in dense smoke; the other thrill was encountered while on my way to Westminster when I was swallowed up in a mob gathered to support a suffragette demonstration. Women dodged the big policemen guarding the entrances, and one of their number leaped over an iron grill. Mounted officers drove the crowd back to the curb, while on the pavement other officers prodded their billies into the backs of the women and ordered them along. Schoolboys in Eton suits watched the excitement from the top of an iron fence. I wanted to go on and get out of it but there was no opening through which to worm my way. Ambulances and patrol-wagons were clanging gongs as they rushed the women to jail. Finally I escaped into the quiet of Westminster, amazed that the calm, controlled women of England could ever be wrought up to such a militant frenzy.

I returned to Liverpool and sailed for Calcutta on the S.S. *City of York,* from whence we journeyed by rail to Gauhati, Assam, at which place we arrived on Christmas Eve, 1910.

IV

ASSAM — THE WETTEST LAND ON EARTH

ASSAM is the most northeastern province of British India. It is wedged between Burma on the south and east, and Bengal on the west. It is a huge tea-garden of rare beauty in the front yard of Tibet and Bhutan. It is one of the wettest places in the world. "Wet," but not in a sense opposite to that in which America is supposed to be dry just now. More rain falls upon the soil of Assam than is recorded for any other section of the earth's surface. The average annual rainfall is from ninety-three to one hundred and twenty-four inches, but in Cherrapunji the average annual fall is four hundred and fifty-eight inches with eight hundred and five actually recorded in one year! This abundant rainfall and melting snows from the Himalayan mountains feed a network of rivers spread out like a spider's web over the country, with the result that Assam has more river-bed per square mile than any other part of the earth's surface.

These rivers nibble their way through fields of rice and sing seawards along rocky mountain-beds fringed with old, gnarled trees bending to see the reflected beauty of trunk and outstretched arms, spilling trailing vines, hanging mosses, ferns and orchids of brown, yellow, pink, lavender and waxen-white with heart of gold. The jungle that carpets low places and hills with bewitchingly verdant beauty affords covert for abundant wild-animal life. Here great herds of wild elephants, tigers, leopards, bears, water-buffaloes, deer, chattering monkeys, the great python, small deadly krite and hooded king-cobra are at home.

In little, brown cottages, usually built with floor and walls of mud and roof of thatch, nestling under clumps of plumed bamboos, in groves of palm and mango trees, live nearly eight million men, women and children. In complexion they range from the African brown of the coolie class to the dark Italian tan of the Zenana women and the people of the hills. In religion nearly half of Assam's millions are Hindus; about one-fifth are Mohammedans and a sixth are animists. The latter are principally Tibeto-Chinese-Burman tribes living in the hills. The Hindus, being Aryans, have the features of the white race; the animists or hill-people have the almond eyes, straight hair and flat noses of the yellow race.

When I first read the life of David Livingstone, that part of the narrative which drove me to my room to hide my face in a pillow, was not the chapters dealing with Livingstone's exploration of rivers and discovery of lakes, but that part of the story which tells of Livingstone's exploration of a black man's heart and his discovery that under skin of black as under the skin of white, beats a heart that " seeking for God, lonely and longing runs." After having lived a dozen years in Assam, meeting men, women and children in their homes, in schools, bazaars and railroads; after having walked with them side by side along highways where white stones check off the miles, or joined their single file along narrow trenches in flooded rice fields where villages counted distance, and through winding jungle paths where rivers crossed and to be crossed, told how much of the journey was yet to be done; after having sat in their court-yards on mats of skin or bamboo and eaten rice and curry from a banana leaf, with my fingers; after having poured tea in china cups for them as they squatted on the floor of my home,—I found that one needs go very lightly indeed, but very lovingly and patiently, to find under skin of brown and tan, as under skin of white and black, a heart that " seeking for God, lonely and longing runs."

On the night of my arrival in Gauhati the Indian Christians gave a reception. The path to the little church was banked on both sides with tall date-palm fronds behind which glimmered rows of little earthen lipped saucers of oil feeding wicks of twisted rag. In the little building used as school-house and church, mine was the fifth adult white face among faces of tan and brown. They spoke a language unintelligible to me. A hymn was announced and I was handed a hymnal printed in

strange characters. Suddenly and keenly I realized
that here I was a stranger and foreigner. Then
the brown people arose to sing, " Joy to the
World," " Room in My Heart for Thee," " What
a Friend We Have in Jesus." Not a word could
I understand, but I knew the songs by their familiar tunes, and by the " light that never was on land
or sea " that beautified those brown faces. I knew
that, after all, I was not a stranger and a foreigner,
but a fellow-citizen with these saints who in an un-
known tongue spoke of experiences common to all
the household of God. That night heart of brown
woman and heart of white woman was one in crying " Abba, Father," and in looking up to God in
praise and love for a common Saviour.

Almost always the first year or two of a foreign
missionary's life is a time of trial and disappointment. Generally loss of weight and a depression
in spirits are accounted for on the score of acclimation. It was so in my case. I did have some
malaria, but there were other things that kept me
awake long hours during the night and made it
difficult for me to swallow food. Naked heathenism at so close range was unspeakably horrid and
repulsive, and there was no escape from it. Every
time I had to pass through the bazaar, I saw
sights that haunted me and kept sleep away at
night. In my language-lessons and study of the
history and customs of the people, I met repulsive
statements that I was not willing at first to accept

A DUG-OUT ON THE KULSI RIVER

SCHOOL GIRLS WEARING THEIR JOPI OR
UMBRELLA

as fact. In all of India there was not a soul that I had ever seen or known before coming to the country,—no one with whom to talk things over.

The only place for laughter and light breathing was in the Tuttle family circle, where Lucile and Stephen in the charm of their childhood helped one to forget. Three months after my arrival the children went to Darjeeling with their mother to attend school in the cool of the hills.

When I had been a little more than a month in Assam, I adopted three little brown girls. This helped some, although the manner of their coming was another horror. Proba and Leci were sisters, five and seven years old. Their mother was a Christian; their father ate hemp, which in its effect is similar to opium. The mother died and the father was negotiating to sell these two little girls, bone of his bone and flesh of his flesh, to a Mohammedan for ten rupees (about three dollars and thirty-five cents). The Mohammedan would have kept the girls as house-servants until they were about thirteen years of age when he would have sold them to some fellow-Mohammedan for wives, receiving forty or even sixty rupees apiece for them. Proba is now married to a Christian and has two children. Leci is completing her training as a nurse, ready to serve in our first woman's hospital, to be opened in Gauhati this winter.

During that first year I took in a little girl about two weeks old. She had been found newly born,

in the bazaar, by sweepers early one morning. Had
the little waif been a boy some sonless sire would
surely have adopted her as his own. In Gauhati, a
town of about 16,000 inhabitants, there is no or-
phanage, no Hindu or Mohammedan hospital for
humans; nor do those who profess these two relig-
ions support the Government hospital except by
providing patients. Yet there is a hospital for
aged, injured and sick cattle, for cows are sacred
to Hindus. So this little discarded mite of hu-
manity was taken to the *thana* (police station).
The baby insisted upon living, yet it could not be
kept at the station. The only door open for this
wee unwanted girlie was down with the women of
shame, and there the policemen took her. After
ten days or so the superintendent of police wrote
me about the baby and asked if I could take her.
At ten o'clock the next morning a policeman came
with three prostitutes, one of whom produced
the baby from the folds of her drapery. The child
was asleep when I took her. One look at the poor
mite made my eyes close to blot out the sight. She
was dressed in three cords on which charms were
strung at her waist and wrists. It was the hot
season before the break of the monsoon,—that
hottest part of the year. I think no one had
cleansed the baby even in mustard oil, from the
hour it was born. Warm oil applied most tenderly
with absorbent cotton left raw, red skin where the
accumulated filth had been. The baby slept

soundly after her bath as I wrapped her in a clean
white swaddling cloth. Five o'clock that afternoon
she had not yet wakened, so I called an old Bible
woman and asked her what was the matter. She
explained that probably before the policeman went
for the baby, the women had given her opium so
as not to be bothered with her crying. One of our
Christian women who yearned for children but had
never known motherhood, later took the baby for
her very own and poured a wealth of love upon it
the one short year of its life.

Native Christians are often another source of
disappointment to the new missionary. In mission
literature and addresses one hears usually of exceptional native Christians—it may be that I
would better say " consecrated " native Christians. Rather foolishly, and yet rather naturally,
one deducts that on foreign mission fields there
are no weak or wavering Christians—none to repre-
sent Judas, or Ananias, but all of the type of John
or Paul or James. But human nature is much the
same all the world over, not only in its yearning
for fellowship with God, but also in its propensity
to sin and failure. In Assam, as in America, I
found Christians of three classes: good, bad, and
indifferent. There, as at home, are to be found
those to whom religion is but a profession. They
make this profession as a fee for which they receive Christian marriage, baptism for their young,

and Christian burial—not bad returns for the investment made.

During my first year in Assam one of our leading educated Christians, the husband of a good wife and father of two children, betrayed the sixteen-year-old motherless daughter of the pastor, while she was looking after four younger children during her father's absence on an evangelistic tour. Other similar cases occurred during those first years. This is the wolf ever at the door of the Indian Christian Church. And ever in his wake is confession with bitter tears, and severance from the body of believers until a new walk in life proves a departure from the old sin. For there is this difference between Christians who live immorally and their Hindu and Mohammedan neighbours who do the same thing: For the Christian it is a violation of his religious precepts and places the offender outside the membership of the Christian Church at least temporarily; whereas for Hindu, Mohammedan and animist, immorality imposes no religious penalty.

In Assam, as in America, I found, also, Christians who have literally " suffered the loss of all things and do count them but refuse that they may win Christ." Listen to the story of Mrinaram, father of Bhuri. Mrinaram was his father's oldest son. The father was the headman of his village. For centuries the oldest son of this house had been the village leader. And in his turn, Mrinaram would succeed his father as headman of the village. The village lay on the north bank of the Brahmaputra River not very far from Gauhati. In order that Mrinaram might be well prepared for his duties, his father sent him to Gauhati to attend high school.

While at high school Mrinaram, one evening in the bazaar, heard of Jesus Christ. He called at the mission bungalow to learn more of Jesus. He found Christ very winsome and almost he was persuaded to become a Christian, but hesitated because the price he must pay was heavy. Later he went to Calcutta to attend the University. While there he was baptized. Such news travels fast even in the jungle, " for a bird of the air shall carry the voice and that which hath wings shall tell the matter." Mrinaram's old father and mother sent for their son. They plead with him to renounce his new faith, undergo the ceremony of being reinstated into caste and let all things be as they had been. They reminded him that if he persisted in the course he had chosen he might not put his shoulder to a burden borne by his old caste-fellows; nor could he drink from the village well, or again eat with his father, or with any of his family or under any caste-roof; neither would he be allowed to settle in the village. His younger brother would succeed to his father's place and patrimony. If Mrinaram persisted in being a

Christian, he would be dead to Hinduism, dead to his village, dead to his home.

Mrinaram's first marriage ceremony with a little girl in the village had been performed. His wife had remained in her father's house expecting the second ceremony to be performed when she was about thirteen, when she would go to her husband's home. When her young husband became a Christian and dead to Hinduism, this little girl automatically became a widow, although she had never lived with her husband. After Mrinaram was adamant to all entreaties to renounce Christ, it was arranged that he might have his wife, hoping that she would win him back to caste. Instead, the young husband won his girl-bride for Christ. As Christians the two young people had no place in their old community so they went out not knowing whither they went. Although the torn hearts of their parents plead for them and suffered with them, they could not lighten the sentence Hinduism imposed upon their children. All that they had known and hoped for, this young couple, a girl of thirteen and a boy of about eighteen, forsook for Christ's sake, " esteeming the reproach for Christ greater riches than the treasures of " Hinduism.

One's fellow-missionaries are sometimes a source of disappointment to the new missionary. When I left America I remembered that my hair was still titian and my temper of the same shade, so

I did not expect the voyage across the ocean to
perfect my saintship. But I did expect other missionaries to be so good that continued contact with
them would effect a decided improvement in me.
I still believe that when the love of Christ con-
trols our words and works and operates in our
lives as we see it operating in the thirteenth of
First Corinthians, no degree of incompatibility of
temper can betray missionaries into saying and
doing some of the unchristian things that some of
the members of our profession have said and done.
I have met a few missionaries whose daily lives
have evinced but little of the graciousness and winsomeness that marked all that Christ did and said,
a few whose spirit and methods seem so little akin
to Christ's that one may but wonder what motive
ever led them into foreign service for Christ.
There is a nimbus to foreign work as viewed from
a distance, a glamour of romance, the appeal of
an opportunity to travel, to meet people of dis-
tinction and achievement, to work at big tasks,—
these things are all alluring and not to be dis-
counted, but together they do not constitute ade-
quate justification for appointment to the ranks of
Christ's ambassadors abroad. Amongst missionaries as amongst physicians, teachers, lawyers,
mechanics, there are misfits. While I cannot deny
that some missionaries have failed wretchedly, I
can testify of many more who have wrought wondrously in the spirit and after the manner of

Christ, and I thank my God upon every remembrance of them.

From many whose lives have been an inspiration and association with whom has been a privilege, let me tell you of one Pitt H. Moore of Nowgong, Assam, who walked worthy of the vocation wherewith he was called. When he first came to Assam, as a young man of twenty-seven, Mr. Moore was the champion tennis-player in the province. His thoughts were direct and expressed in chaste, lucid English. He found the study of Assamese difficult at first and was slower than most missionaries to begin to use the language. But he afterwards became so expert in the use of the vernacular, that when the Assamese heard his voice but could not see the speaker, they supposed they were listening to a fellow-countryman using their mother-tongue. When this man had served in Assam for more than thirty years and had developed statesman-like qualities that made his judgment of mission problems of great value, I was privileged to spend some months in his home. Not for an equal number of years' training in any institution that I know of, would I exchange those months of fellowship with this ideal missionary.

His home was an old bungalow that had been built in 1850, with trees carried from the jungle by elephants. Not a nail was used in its construction, the material being tied with beth (pronounced bet[h]), the outer

fibre of cane. It was much the worse for wear
and in need of alterations and repairs; one and
two inch cracks separated some of the roughly-
planed floor-planks; bats infested the spaces between the thatch roof and cloth ceilings, coming
into the house at nightfall, flying about the rooms
and fastening themselves to the mosquito curtains
over our beds. The bungalow was not screened.
Dozens of little house-lizards sported about the
whitewashed walls, now still as death, now quick
as lightning in a dart for mosquitoes. But the old
place was cool and comfortable; it was rich in
associations; it was loved by the Assamese, and
Mr. and Mrs. Moore were quite content with it,
although they generously seconded requests from
younger missionaries for more comfortable and
more elaborate dwellings. In all things this fine
missionary was most generous with others, but
carefully guarded personal expenditure and was
conspicuously economical in the use of mission
funds.

Mr. Moore's day began early and the freshest,
best bit of it was spent in his study. At six we
had early breakfast. After breakfast he was busy
with teachers and preachers from the district, the
sick coming for medicines, the perplexed for advice, the sorrowing for comfort. A great part of
the morning was spent sawing, planing, and ham-
mering on the school-building that he had designed,
gathered the material for and was building with

only unskilled native help, working side by side
with coolies and mechanics. In a rare degree he
possessed those two virtues without which one
may not profitably serve in India—love and patience. After the noon-meal we had prayers.
Then the mission builder and statesman was a
little child, simple, direct, confident in his fellowship with his Father; a householder with the needs
of family and friends on his heart, a shepherd concerned for his flock, an ambassador reporting to
his King and asking for instructions.

Frequently we differed on questions of mission
policy, and in his capacity as Chairman of our
Mission Reference Committee, Mr. Moore had to
vote against a measure upon which he knew that
I had set my heart. I accepted his veto without
question, remembering the old prayer-times and
grateful for the friendship of one so true to his
Master and to his interpretation of wise methods,
that not even the desire to please a young missionary in whom he was interested as in a daughter, could deflect his vote. This man of rare gifts
gave of his best as unstintingly to the poorest tea-
garden coolie that came his way as he did to the
highest government official or the most promising
or most trying missionary. Yet was not the gift
appreciated by the native church in Nowgong.
The history of this church was not unlike that of
the young church at Corinth, as may be gleaned
from Paul's first letter to them. There was among

them " envying, and strife and divisions," and this burden of the church broke their leader's health and heart.

Tenderly his brother carried him down to Calcutta where skilful surgeons tried to discover the seat of his trouble. They could find no disease nor organic disorder; neither could they stay the ebbing life. When missionaries and native Christians from all over Assam were gathered together in Nowgong for a conference for which Mr. Moore had made preparations, news of the good man's going Home was received by wire. A thousand men and women sobbed together; from the corners, the center, the rear and front of the great grass tabernacle, proud men arose crushed, humbled and penitent, declaring that they had killed him with their false pride, that they had broken his heart with their waywardness; leaders of factions in the strife and divisions, sought one another and begged forgiveness; secret sins were confessed, a better life was pledged and the burden of every man's sob was, " He loved me so, and I didn't deserve it; now I can never repay him."

A grave was dug in the well-kept English cemetery where are laid to rest a few score planters, officials and missionaries. A prominent Mohammedan of the town sought for audience with those in charge of the funeral arrangements and begged that the ashes be laid, not amongst foreign but with the Indian dead, " for," said the Mohammedan,

" he lived for us; he lived most of his life with us; he died for us; let him be buried with us. He would so have had it." Even so was it done, for when the brother returned from Calcutta with the urn of ashes, he said that some time before his illness Mr. Moore had requested that in the event of his death, he be rolled in a bamboo mat and buried in the native Christian cemetery. So the Hindus claimed him in his cremation, and Mohammedans and Christians in his burial.

The day of the funeral, schools, court-house and government offices were closed and Hindu, Mohammedan and Christian officials and coolies, joined in loving tribute and walked in the procession to the open field where the Christian dead are buried. There in a flower-lined grave they placed the ashes of Pitt H. Moore, who had loved them unto the end. So passed the missionary-hero who did not strive nor cry; neither did any man hear his voice in the streets. A bruised reed did he not break, and smoking flax did he not quench, but in love and patience, like Enoch of old, " he walked with God and was not, for God took him." This type of Christian worker and lover is the dominant type on every mission-field.

But more than in any native Christian or fellow-missionary, is the young missionary apt to be disappointed in himself. With at least a fair degree of training, with high and holy hope, he dedicates himself and all his abilities to a high task. He goes forth yearning for an opportunity to sacrifice, to burn out in service for Christ. He is sometimes disappointed to find himself housed in a comfortable, screened bungalow rather than the rude shelter he had imagined would be his home. He is inclined to be impatient with the measure of social formalities imposed by residence in a European colony of officials, planters, and commercial men, when he longs for more time to establish points of contact with the natives. He chafes against mission red-tape as an untrained colt chafes at bridle and saddle. He frets under restrictions necessitated by an Oriental attitude toward sex. His patience is ravelled by native procrastination and sloth. He rebels against established methods, resents the Easterner's dislike of change, and even more fiercely resents every semblance of Orientalism that stamps his fellows long-resident in the country. Perhaps most of all he dislikes the general European attitude towards these subject brown people. Tasks multiply and more and more little duties that he had not counted on, drain the time and strength dedicated to the great task, and encroach upon the time he had set aside for quiet and communion with his Lord.

Then there comes a night in the valley of humiliation. He realizes that he has failed: failed to learn of those he came to teach; failed to profit by the wisdom of those long-experienced in the

task; failed to remain entirely free of the patron-
izing manner he so keenly resented when he first
detected it in others. He knows that sentient
hands of brown men have handled him, that nothing has escaped the calm eyes that have been taking his measure, or the patient ears that have
sounded his depth. He knows that in patience
and love and understanding, he has failed brown
brother and white colleague,—that as he was disappointed in them, so, too, have they been disappointed in him. " They made me the keeper of
the vineyards: but mine own vineyard have I not
kept." Slowly stars of promise and resolve
lighten the gloom until a morning of clearer vision
dawns. He sees that the big task is made up of
small duties done in a noble way; that the sacri-
fices to be made are not necessarily of a sanitary
house and many of the comforts of life, but the
more subtle sacrifice of cherished ideas and personal opinions; that not always is the missionary
called to the loneliness and privation of Livingstone's pioneer career, but often is challenged to
live in Christian love and fellowship, in close quarters with other strong natures not in all things in
accord with his own. As he mingles with those
in the European colony he finds that there are
white men, too, on his foreign field with hearts
feeling after God. He comes to regard mission
red-tape as a necessary voucher for well-meaning
folk in the homeland who question the wisdom and

honesty of their representatives abroad. He sees
that in this foreign land he has much to learn as
well as much to teach. Brightest of all the lights
in this new dawn is the conviction that there need
be no more nights in the valley of humiliation if
part of every day is spent alone with Him in
Whose service he is engaged.

The establishment of a kindergarten and boarding department occupied most of my first term of
service. The purpose of the kindergarten was to
try to wedge into the indifference of Hinduism and
Mohammedanism, seemingly untouched after seventy years of mission work. The boarding-school
was designed to gather for training in Christian
living, home-making, and school-work, some of the
most promising girls from the little Christian villages in the foot-hills forty-two to seventy miles
from Gauhati.

The old Indian boarding-school* was harshly
criticised as a denationalizing institution. In the
old schools the students were usually housed in a
single large dormitory with cement floors; they
slept on iron cots, their food was prepared in one
portion for the whole school and their clothing was
sent outside to be laundered. Many of our Christian evangelists and teachers preferred to marry

* The substance of what appears on this, and the two following pages, is contained in a booklet entitled *Satribari
School* which I wrote for distribution by The Board of Missionary Cooperation, Northern Baptist Convention.—E. M. H.

uneducated girls rather than take a wife whose training in such a boarding-school unfitted her for happy, helpful living in the typical Indian home— a little house of mud walls and floor, beds of bamboo and a rounded hole in the ground for a stove. The old boarding-school girl did not know how to keep the mud floors beautiful with the smear of thin mud; after having slept some years on a woven spring mattress, she was not easily reconciled to the hard bamboo bed; neither did she know how to cook in small family portions, nor how to keep the clothing of her household clean. Trying to overcome these difficulties, we grouped our students into families and provided for them in typical Indian fashion.

Just within the Gauhati municipal boundary, we secured about twenty-six acres of land on part of which we built a small model Christian village, with typical Indian homes, thatch roof, mud floors and walls, bamboo beds, etc. Each cottage has two bedrooms of six beds each and two occupants to a bed. The center or third room of each cottage is a living-room or study-room. This living-room is common to the two families occupying the cottage. Each family has its own little storeroom for vegetables and the weekly supply of rice, also a room in the cook-shed where the meals are prepared and eaten. Ten or twelve girls constitute a family. One of the number, an older girl, is chosen as house-mother, and another, house-auntie.

The house-mother is responsible for the expenditure of the weekly allowance for vegetables and for the assignment and proper performance of the cooking, cleaning and general work of the house and yard. Other important members of the family group are the babies and their mothers. For each family has a family baby—sometimes a babe in arms, sometimes a couple of months or more than a year old. The babies are the most important part of the scheme. They have done more than any other agency for the development of the beautiful in our girls. The baby-mother is responsible for feeding, bathing, and the general care of her little one, dressing and putting her to bed, washing and mending for her. Faithlessness to her trust entails its forfeiture both for house mothers and baby mothers. Over all the families, as a sort of grandmother, is a capable, understanding Indian Christian widow, the mother of thirteen children of her own. When, as frequently happens, a young man comes to the school seeking for a wife, I always considered as ineligible those girls that have failed to show interest in or love for the babies in the school or have in any way neglected the little ones committed to their care. There is a very healthy and helpful rivalry between the various baby mothers and also between the various house mothers and families for the best prepared food, the neatest house, the shiniest brass vessels in the cook-house, the trimmest gar-

dens, tidiest personal appearance, etc. The plan
has worked wonderfully well. It has been followed in our new mission boarding-school at Golo-
ghat and has met with unstinted praise and the
unqualified approval of the Indians, missionaries
and government. But most of all is it commended
by the fruit it has produced in the lives of the
girls.

In that first term there were several thrilling
experiences that I had all but forgotten until I
read the following letters that my home folk failed
to consign to the waste-paper basket:

Gauhati,
(8) May, 1913.

Dear Nettie:

I'd give much to have you see the Indian jug-
glers. They are clever! About ten days ago we
had one do his tricks for boarders and day pupils.
This fellow was as good as I have seen. He made
smoke and fire come from his mouth, not for a
second, but for fully two minutes. I tried to snap
it, but it was among my blistered films. He did
more than half of his tricks on the schoolmaster,
which added to their interest for the children.
He showed us a round tin box with a funnel-
shaped top. We all looked into it. The schoolmaster stuck his nose in. It was empty; it was
sound and without an inner lining, so far as we
could judge. The juggler filled it with water and

then poured water out and poured it out, but the box remained always full and overflowing. The pundit saw that the box was still full of water and fastened the lid on. Then he held his hand out when the juggler immediately turned the can upside down, pulled off the lid, but instead of the water and splash that we expected, out came a snake and shriek when the pundit felt it in his hand. The snake was put back and the lid put on, but when it was pulled off again, instead of a snake there were quantities of fragrant temple lilies,—so many tumbled out that they had to be jammed to get into the tin again. For an hour we enjoyed other tricks just as wonderful and knew that three rupees was good pay for the performer.

Nowgong, Assam.

Dear Friend-Who-Couldn't-Come:

. . . Last week I had another ox-cart ride. Mrs. Kampfer did not really need me any longer, as she and the baby are doing nicely, so I went back to Nowgong, taking Profulla with me. Profulla means Gladness, and this chubby child of four or five years is well named. She seems a composite of the ripple and gurgle of the streams of the hill country in which she was born and of the warmth and glow of the sunlight of the plains where she has flirted and frolicked through the years of babyhood. The resultant is a charming mixture of quiet shyness streaked with short seasons of cuddling and affection; reserve and wide distance maintained with strangers but a winsome familiarity and outpouring of confidential chatter for those whom she elects as friends. The child's voice possesses such rare sweetness, that often I lose the sense of her rambles by listening to their music. Profulla's almond eyes set in a broad flat face proclaim her Mongolian descent. She is a Naga,—a tribe of fearless hill-people living at China's back door.

We left Gauhati about noon of an intolerably hot day. For six hours we sat on the sunny side of the railway carriage. An Eurasian bridal couple sat on the shady side of the carriage and they annoyed me even more than the heat. Not because they had the shady side of the carriage, but because they sat at the extreme ends of the seat with seating room for three or four between them. Although Profulla, busy with the sights to be seen from the windows, politely turned her back to her fellow-passenngers and I buried myself in a magazine, nevertheless that bridal couple sat not one mite closer! In six hours, they exchanged exactly six remarks; it may be that they had limited themselves to one remark an hour, for both bride and groom wore wrist-watches which they studiously scanned every few minutes.

At Chaparmuk we changed from the railroad carriage to the ox-cart. Mr. Moore was at the station to see us safely in the cart before he took

the train for upper Assam. My suitcase and par-
cels were stowed in front of the cart behind the
driver's seat and Profulla and I climbed into the
back of the cart. The driver, a mere boy, yoked
the oxen, and we jolted on our way. When a
friendly cloud hid the sun we scrambled from the
cart and walked several miles under wonderful
sunset clouds with lights and shadows playing on
field and jungle, clothing the Mikir Hills with
that indescribable blue haze with which Nature
weaves evening dress for her high places. While
the sky still retained some of the glow of evening
embers, Venus sparkled pure and gold in her bed
of blue: almost immediately every vestige of
colour disappeared from the clouds, leaving Venus'
bright rays to reflect fallen gems in every stream
and flooded place. Other stars were faintly
twinkling; Arcturus was sliding down the western horizon hard upon the lost sun; Vega and
Altair were shining bright and clear west of the
zenith where the cross of Cygnus was spread.
There was no moon. Before Auriga was well over
the east it became densely dark, seemingly in a
moment. We had walked quite a distance, so
climbed into the cart again.

Profulla chatted until she fell asleep. Then I
wanted more than ever to get out and watch the
lightning as it tore livid rents in the black sky.
I leaned from the cart ready to jump when I
thought about snakes. I do not know just what

effect storms have upon these gliding creatures, and it was very, very dark, except when the lightning flashed. Much as I love storms in the open, more do I fear snakes in the dark, so I stayed in the cart. That was a regal storm such as frequently marks the end of the monsoon. For hours the thunder cannonaded with echoing rumbles in the hills. The lightning was vividly sharp and almost incessant. It struck trees which crashed to the ground in beds of broken branches and twigs. After the fury of the storm had abated, the rain came in torrents. Wind, thunder and lightning still raged with tropic passion, but not with the madness of the first onslaught. Exhausted by the excitement of the day, Profulla slept soundly. We must have been in the storm several hours, when one of the oxen threw the yoke and in doing so, set the cart at right angles with the road. We were backed towards a body of water which I supposed was a flooded rice-field. The cart wheels were perilously near the edge of the bank. If the cart should receive the slightest impetus in that direction, it would roll down into the water. The driver was dancing on the fork of the cart trying to reach the balky beast with a stick. If he continued such capers, either he or the oxen would have us in the water or turned over in the mud. The only vernacular I can speak is Assamese, and as yet I'm not very fluent in that. The driver spoke only Hindustani and could not understand

Assamese. I called to him to jump to the ground to manage his beasts. Of course he did not understand me. I straddled Profulla across my hip, after the Assamese fashion of carrying their young, and started for the front of the cart, intending to jump to the ground.

Just then the boy pulled the balking ox against the cart with a thud. The other ox slipped from under the yoke and sent the cart rolling down, down, the bank into the water. Incidentally it put out the lantern which had hung from the bottom of the cart, and left us in dense darkness, except for the lightning. The tongue of the cart was embedded in the slime and mud of the bank. An ox-cart is quite high even when standing level, and our baggage, placed in the front of the cart, tilted it towards the tongue, so raising the back of the wagon; nevertheless water came into the cart at the back. There was a strong, swift, storm-fed current. It was not a rice-field, but a river,—the Noi Kolung—freighted with the debris of the storm. Flashes of lightning showed that it was quite wide. It was impossible to stay in the cart. At any moment it might assume its natural position when unyoked, and tip backwards in spite of the baggage weighting the front. I did not relish the prospects of being dumped in a heap out into the river, with a little one to care for and probably some baggage beside the mattress and cart tumbled on top of us. The wind rendered the umbrella useless even if we could have bothered with it. Our clothing was already saturated. The driver sat at the head of the cart wailing as only an Oriental can. I climbed over the baggage, carrying Profulla pig-a-back, walked on the tongue of the cart through the water to the bank. Time and again while climbing the clay bank we slipped back grasping a broken twig or a handful of up-rooted grass and mud, but finally, muddy and drenched, we reached the road.

The lightning revealed clusters of banana-trees and betel-palms in the distance. In the jungle, banana and betel trees are signs of habitation, so we started in the direction of the sighted trees, Profulla walking alongside and clinging to my skirts as she scolded the driver. Only once when the lightning was unusually sharp, she clung to my skirts and begged to be carried. When the lightning flashed we would run as far as it revealed the way. In the dark we stood still and waited. Deep puddles flooded the jungle-path, but we waded right through them, for we were already drenched and a little more wet did not matter.

The first path branching from the road seemed to lead nowhere, but the lightning revealed buildings beyond us, so we returned to the road and took the second path which led to a little native hut and two unwalled bullock sheds. We knocked at the bamboo door and called and called, explaining that our cart had been backed into the river

CROSSING THE BOKO RIVER IN A QUEEN'S
CHAIR

"MY FOUR ADOPTED BROWNIES"

and we were seeking shelter from the storm. We waited what seemed a long time but no answer came, although we heard voices within. The driver must have been frightened after we left him, for after a while he appeared in the bullock shed and knocked on the hut door saying many things in Hindustani. But the door remained shut and the hut was still dark. The bullock shed was tiny, crowded with bullocks, and leaked, so the earthen floors were a sorry mess. Voices were again heard in the hut and a ray of light showed through a hole made in the bamboo door for a chain. We renewed our appeals and waited. Finally the door opened a little way and a frightened man with a little lamp held in the shade of his hand asked in Assamese what we wanted. At the sound of Assamese I gathered confidence and courage, for I know the vernacular well enough to understand all that he said and to make myself understood after a fashion. Sometimes more than a common means of speech is necessary to understanding, however, and it was so in this case. I could not understand that under such circumstances one human being should have to beg another for aid and that it would be denied seemed incredible. But this man would not let us into his house. He would not help the cartman with the cart. He would help in the morning if I gave him a rupee. Then I asked for a lantern or light of some kind. He did not have a lantern. The native lamp that he held in his hand was a little cup cut from empty kerosene tins, with tiny tin pipe-stem opening in the center of the top through which the rag wick is drawn. When I asked him for one of these, he appeared with another of the little shadeless tins that sell for a cent each and said that he would lend us one, but how was he to know that we would return it. I had no money but remembered my cameo ring. I took it off and thrusting it at the man told him that it was worth many rupees and hundreds of tin lamps. Still holding the lamp, he put the ring as far on his hand as it would go. In a rage I seized upon the lamp and shouted above the storm, " You're a mean, mean man! Sometime you will be in trouble and I hope many, many people will help you and make you ashamed of yourself for your meanness to us tonight." In my excitement I mixed English and Assamese indiscriminately. The fellow may have thought I cursed him. He declared himself to be a good man, drew the ring from his finger, said he did not want it and insisted upon my taking it back.

We carried the lamp back to the cart, the wind blowing it out on the way. There were only two matches left in the driver's store. Because of the wind blowing the lamp we could not stay under the trees. We had to risk the cart which was still upright. Drawing the baggage a little further toward the front, Profulla and I sat on it to help

weight the forepart of the cart. Finding the
driver's tobacco box (an empty condensed milk
can) hanging to the side of the cart at the front,
I threw the tobacco into the river and dropped the
lamp into the empty can to protect it from the
wind. The wick above the pipe stem had burned
out, the flame flickered and we were again in darkness and without matches. Suddenly I remembered having part of a box of matches in my handbag, I did not dare risk tilting the cart by reach-
ing back for the bag, but fished for it with the tip
of my umbrella. Fortunately, it was a leather bag
lined with dog skin; though the outside of the bag
was soaked the box of matches was dry. There
were about a dozen matches in it. We pinched the
burnt wick, put the lamp back into the empty can
and relighted it.

Suddenly the storm calmed somewhat. It still
rained, but not torrentially; the lightning was no
longer sharp; the wind did not blow. The driver
started off gesticulating as he poured forth vol-
umes of Hindustani. I had no idea as to what he
meant to do, where he was going or why. Neither
did I know where we were. In the Noi Kolung,
of course, but in what part of the Noi Kolung?
We might have been just outside Nowgong or only
half-way there. I did not know whether it was
midnight or nearly morning. The sky gave no
promise of dawn though the twilight seemed ages
past. I knew that the little lamp could not burn

much longer. Profulla shivered with the cold. I wrapped her in the driver's wet blanket for it was the driest thing at hand. Then we waited. Every kind of creature seemed disturbed. There were heavy splashes in the river all around us. They might have been caused by dropping brush or by fish, but they might just as well have been crocodiles or sharks, so I kept the closed umbrella in my hand pointed at the rear cart opening, determined that anything that might swim into the back of the cart should swallow the umbrella before it did us. The water noises seemed to be augmented. Black shapes glided down the river. It would be better to wait on land even without the light. But just then jackals came howling and yelling that weird cry that savours so strangely of the laugh-sob of hysterics. The pack came yelping nearer than I cared to hear them. Frogs croaked. A bird gave a shrill shriek. I pictured it being stung by a snake. After all, it was probably safer in the cart. Profulla went to sleep again on my lap. Slowly the time dragged on while I pondered what men did and how they lived before fire and artificial lights were used. The intermittent gleam of fireflies showed beautifully in the dark that brooded over land and water.

Then I began to think how very much worse things might have been: had the cart tilted backwards into the water, had there been no matches in the handbag, had there been no hut near the road, had there been a hungry tiger in the jungle (for this is famous tiger territory). Then the funny side of the affair began to appear. How terrified you home-folk would be if you could know of my plight! What would you not give for a glimpse of me huddled in a corner of such a queer houseboat, with a brown baby snugly sleeping in my arms! I smiled broadly in the dark. Time passed more quickly. The sounds were not so alarming as they had been. Prospects were not hopeless. The experience would afford lots of fun afterwards. Why, it seemed like being a really truly missionary, with " journeyings often, in perils of water, in perils in the wilderness, in weariness, in watchings often." No, on the whole it was not half bad, and—

The driver came back with a cart and a hurricane lantern with but little oil in it and a chimney so filthy that only a flicker of light could pierce through. The cart had nothing but broken nail-heads over the rough, bare floor, but it seemed luxurious. A bullock cart passed and we called to the driver for help, but his only reply was to drive a little faster. With difficulty we transferred the suitcase to the new cart and started for Nowgong, leaving the cart, mattress and other things to their fate. We reached our journey's end as the clock struck four.

Though Profulla had seemed not at all phased by the storm, she lost her nerve when taken out to the dormitory where about fifty strange little brown girls were sleeping, and would not be pacified until allowed to come into the bungalow and sleep on a pallet near the one she knew.

That was the most destructive storm of the season. Many large trees on the mission compound had been destroyed, and the town was littered with fallen trees and uprooted brush. The next day the cart was rescued. I had several notes of condolence from friends who grieved that I had met such a severe storm on the road, but never dreamed that I had spent part of the night on (or was it in?) the Noi Kolung.

V

SOME LETTERS FROM THE FIELD

I PROPOSE to devote practically this entire chapter to letters written home at various times. They describe intimately the various experiences which were mine at the time they were written, and have the value of being impressions of the time rather than observations made in long retrospect:

April 6, 1913.

My Dear Ones:

If you could look in on us this morning you would wonder what has happened. Curtains and pictures down, tables and chairs piled up, soaked rugs spread out-of-doors, school furniture and supplies piled on the veranda, the children's things hanging all about, the organ with its leather cover curled up ready to shed and the wood crinkled as with a curling iron. All these things piled on the back veranda as in a storage room for rubbish, the other parts of the house without a stick of furniture, yard of drapery or bit of carpet, but floors covered with the muddy tracks of boots and brooms, the walls drenched and the wet plaster making the place ill-smelling. You see we had a tornado Saturday night. Some of the hailstones, weighed afterwards on the scales, were a quarter to a half-pound each. They pelted our asbestos roof and riddled it like so many bullets. The torrents poured through these holes and came through the ceiling at such a rate that walking through the front rooms was like walking through a drenching rain. The wind tore the screening from the front veranda, uprooted great trees and twisted off the branches of others as though they had been so many pieces of pottery. The schoolhouse roof was lifted on one side, curled as hair around a finger, and thrown off to the side. Then the stones punched holes in the 4 x 6 foot composition blackboard that we had made last week, and the wind wrenched it from its frame and hurled it out-of-doors like useless chaff. A large supply wardrobe was thrown on its face. The supports for the flower-boxes in the kindergarten gave way and the boxes fell,—kindling and soil mixing with broken glass, fallen pictures and torn curtains, in one grand, hasty pudding.

At the very beginning of the havoc, the lightning tossed about fifteen feet off the top of a huge teak tree between the house and the girls' cottage, as one flecks a crumb from a table. As it fell the tree crashed against the wall of the girls' house, knocking it in just where the girls sleep. Fortunately, their heads were on the inner end of their pallets. The mothers grabbed their babies, the bigger girls took the smaller ones and rushed down stairs. Four of the girls were in the bungalow with me and when the storm started and the tree crashed Proba rushed over to the bungalow, but we could scarcely force the door of the screen-porch open to let her in. She was only a foot or two from me and I yelled with all my strength, but the hail had set in with such din, while the thunder, crashing trees and falling glass made so much noise that we couldn't hear our own voices. The hailstones fell with such force that they rebounded from the ground and it seemed that lightning and hail both were coming up from the earth as well as down from above.

When I could get out to the cottage the girls were all huddled together, the larger girls carrying the smaller ones. The matron and many of the larger girls were weeping hysterically, but the little children were wide-eyed, but quiet and without sign of a tear. In the bungalow we were like drowned rats with the water above our ankles, so we couldn't bring the girls in here. Just as soon as the storm permitted them to get out, Mr. Stephen and the coachman came to see if we were all right and what they could do to help us out. We went over to the Stephen bungalow and slept there, or rather lay down on the floor and talked until it was light enough to get out and see what damage had been done. We were hardly settled in the bungalow when the chief Government official came to see if there were any casualties on our compound. It is a marvel that but five people were killed by falling houses or pelting stones. Many were bruised with the hailstones, but were saved serious injury by crawling under the bamboo beds when the stones cut through the thatch roof.

The next morning we were up at dawn, and such havoc on all sides! Half of the big trees on our compound were down, and all through the town there were so many uprooted trees that they had to dynamite them and get a couple hundred prisoners out to clear them from the roads. A great rubber tree in which a community of flying foxes stay, crashed to the ground killing several score of these loathsome, ill-smelling creatures that are neither bird nor beast. Frogs and rats lay where a stone had struck them. Birds were wailing for their nests and young. The ground bore deep pockmarks of hail. The poor houses of the coolie class were heaped piles of rubbish, their occupants happily fishing in the flooded gutters and fields, or gathered in groups reporting their feelings and experiences of the night before and agreeing that not even from their fathers' fathers had they ever heard of such a storm. Some people prayed that night who do not usually have evening prayers.

The roads were impassable for wheeled vehicles, but we saddled our ponies, went over or around the heaps of debris in the road, and looked up most of our outside school children to see if any were in distress. We think that the storm was quite local and that none of our other stations were hurt.

Gauhati,
Feb. 3, 1913.

. . . Last week an anxious mother came to inquire why her boy plays so much in school and is whipped so little! Last week I was out two afternoons visiting in the homes and hearing the chorus, " Whip them more, Missahib!" This afternoon I was talking to my perpetually bad girl. The only good she does is in promising, but there is something about the child that I love. I stood her in a corner this afternoon and when I was talking with her after school, trying to show her the folly of making promises only to break them and telling her that she could not come to school unless she behaves and lets those around her behave, she told me with sober sobbing that if I would only whip her hard she might be good! Wonderful East!

Zenana Mission House,
Darjeeling,
August 12, 1913.

Dear Home-folk:

. . . Have I written you about our trip to see the sunrise on Everest? I don't mean that we went to Everest, but last Wednesday morning I was up at quarter past one and waited until quarter of four for my pony and the rest of the party.

I had a splendid spirited pony that was so impatient to go that he wouldn't be still while I mounted, so I had to gallop off with my stirrup a little too short. Oh, but it was a glorious ride— uphill most of the way. The beast went like the wind, leaving the others one by one, quite far behind. I guess he doesn't often have a burden as light as eighty-nine pounds to carry. There was a wind stirring and enough sharpness in the air to make one's blood tingle. As we galloped through the cantonments at Jalaphar the sentinel challenged me, but I hadn't time to shout, "I'm going to Tiger Hill," before the pony was off madly, again. Just as the morning star dimmed I crossed the little settlement at Ghoom, which lies between the hill I had crossed and the one I had yet to climb. I feared the pink of dawn would appear before I reached the hilltop, so I let the pony have the lines and go his own pace. He, too, seemed possessed by the spirit of the morning so galloped most of the way.

When we reached the observation platform on top of the hill, the sky was aglow and the nearer snows shone between two banks of clouds. . . . Dawn flooded the plains below with their great swollen rivers lying like thin strands of silver across the land. The grand line of snow peaks was covered with every roseate shade and flecked with gold and hints of green. The clouds shifted and moved sometimes in filmy mists, sometimes

in huge masses, with white fleecy bits snuggled
here and there on great mountain bosoms, all con-
tinually changing shape and catching different
colours. We watched the shifting masses until
the sun was quite strong. Kanchanjanga was ma-
jestic, so dazzlingly white in the sun that she
seemed a great scintillating jewel. But Everest
did not show that morning. I was sorry, for some
who watched with us will probably not have another opportunity to see this peerless peak, and
were but little consoled when those of us who have
seen it, explained that from this point of observation, it can not compare in grandeur with any of
the dozen glistening crowns that we were looking at.

Timi, Sikim, India,
October 6, 1913.

Dear Ones at Home:
    . . . Eighteen miles on my circuitous trip home
to Gauhati. Timi is twenty-six miles from Darjeeling. The road is as many miles of every
variety of beauty. We left Darjeeling, Thursday
about four P. M. and were entertained at a tea-
garden about six miles out, or rather down, for
the road was all down hill, and in some places so
steep that there were stone stairways. Of course
we didn't ride over these, but it was too grotesque
to see the syces leading the ponies down. After a
bit the poor creatures' ankles knocked together so

that you would think they couldn't go on. We had sent the coolies on ahead with our baggage, but when we arrived at Mrs. Shannon's we found that the coolies had not yet come. It was about seven and quite dark except for good starlight. We had tea according to the English custom of refreshing guests, and sat on the veranda until eight, waiting for the coolies, for knowing that these people dress for dinner we had each packed a dinner-dress. But when the baggage hadn't come at eight, we went to our room, washed up and put back our soiled clothes for dinner.

The English seem to go in for silver so much more than we do, but do not use cut-glass as much, probably because the servants break so much. They serve their meals in delightful style. After dinner we had a few games and then to bed. In the morning we walked around the garden before breakfast, and such a lovely garden it was! The shady side of the hill faces the snows, and here Mr. Shannon has set out masses of ferns and orchids. It is one of the most beautiful bits of garden I have ever seen. These people are very fond of their garden; both of them are botanists. They watch the birds and have learned about them; they collect butterflies; they entertain those who cannot return their hospitality. After breakfast Mr. Shannon walked with us several miles through his garden on to the Government road. Then the way lay through a forest, and such but-

terflies we saw! Large as birds, some seemed;
some were black with bars of white and other
colours, some brilliantly hued.

As we continued downhill it became warmer and
warmer until we reached the river that separates
Bengal from Sikim. Here we mounted the horses
that had been sent on before, and started up the
mountain on the other side of the river. About
four o'clock we reached the dak bungalow where
we were to spend the night. It is the great puja
time, when most natives work little and drink
much. The coolies had left the bridge before us
and should have reached the bungalow shortly
after we did. After having waited for them more
than an hour, we decided to go to the bazaar and
try to find something to eat as we had had nothing since morning. A crowd of curious people
tagged after us in the bazaar, but no one could
tell us where we might get fruit or eggs, so we
went back to the bungalow empty-handed, washed
our hands without soap, dried them on our petti-
coats, and went to bed. I woke up to hear dishes
rattle. The coolies had arrived and we ate and
ate, and drank and drank.

After the cool of Darjeeling, the place seemed
close and stuffy. There was but one window; the
door was half off its hinges. Knowing that the
natives were all drinking and that we were the
only Europeans anywhere about, I took two big
hat-pins and put them by my pillow. Neither of

us slept very much. We were up about six in the morning, had breakfast, packed the bedding and left the village about nine. The rest of the journey lay almost entirely through forests. It was shady and got cooler and cooler as we ascended. About noon we came to the second valley and began another descent. This road was darker and damper than the one we had come. It was too hard on the ponies to ride them down such steep grades, so we dismounted and fed them while waiting for the syces to come. Then we saw that we had stirred up leeches. One pony had about twenty around his mouth and ever so many others on his head and feet. We, too, had the things pacing their queer way over our boots. Between the soles and about the tongue they had made their way inside. We daren't sit down to take off our shoes, so one supported the other while we hunted out the clingers. The last of the walk downhill was very wearying so tea, served as soon as we arrived, was very refreshing.

The place here is beautiful. The snows are nearer than at Darjeeling. The second range that we see from our bedroom is snow-capped. In front of the house is a high hill across a narrow valley through which a stream flows as a silver girdle. On either side of the foremost hill are spurs and saddles of several ranges. Here the clouds perpetually chase light and shade; it is ever varying, always lovely. Mrs. MacKean, our hos-

tess, fits wonderfully well in this mountain setting.
She is big in her spirit, natural in her manner and
an ideal helpmeet for a lonely frontier missionary.
There is a little girl almost six and as interesting
as free life in these marvelous hills can make a
child who has wise, cultured parents.

Gauhati, Assam,
Feb. 17, 1914.

You Dear-People-Who-Are-Home:

. . . I've just concluded one of the most interesting of all my interesting experiences. I've been
out in the district! . . . I didn't get my home
letter off last week, because there is only a weekly
post from the place where we were, and that was
too late for the foreign mail. In fact the post
never finds Barigaon, the village where we stayed
for the Association, but the men carry the mail
once a week about eight miles into the bazaar, and
get the village mail for the week at the same time.

I took our big girl, Sumuri, and the baby and
left here Tuesday about three P. M. About fifteen miles out Isabelle met us with the American
wagon. We rested at the dak bungalow for the
night and were up the next morning at four-thirty
and away on the road again by six. There is only
one seat, and the baggage occupies the back of the
wagon, so we took turns riding on the seat and on
the baggage. We passed scores of people carrying, on either end of a long shoulder-stick, bamboo

baskets of greens, silk cocoons, pottery and other
wares, to a large weekly bazaar in a nearby tea-
garden.

About one o'clock we came to the river where
we transferred ourselves and baggage into a dug-
out, i. e., a hollowed tree-trunk, and made the
rest of the journey by water. It is when I am seeing beautiful bits of country that I fairly ache to
have you at home see them with me. It is not
when things are sad or hard that I am smitten with
loneliness, but when there is something glad or
beautiful, that I yearn to have you share it with
me. . . . There are low, dipping foothills on both
sides of the river, and more or less jungle on the
skirting road. At first the midday glare marred
perfect enjoyment, but later in the afternoon the
hills cast long shadows on the water and draped
themselves in purple, the wild cocks crowed as
they went to nest, and mating birds singing vespers made the evening melodious. It was moonlight when we landed on the sands of Barigaon
and a short walk across the sandy stretch brought
us to the village proper and to dear faithful
Rhanji with supper ready to be served.

They had built us a basha of grass and bamboos, of one large room with the back screened off
by grass and built up with a bamboo platform
with a layer of rice straw on top. This platform
was at once our bed and bedroom. The front of
the grass partition served as living- and dining-

room. Here, too, a carpet of straw protected us from the cold earth. Whenever our living-room failed to accommodate the crowds that visited us, the people on the outside parted the dried grass walls with their hands and thrust their heads through. Our living-room opened onto our bathroom, a little grass room about as large as a good-sized packing-case and without a lid. One side of this was furnished with a little bamboo platform that served as bathtub. We stood on this and poured water over our soaped bodies. Oh, it was life in the rough, but it was interesting!

My heart yearned for the women and children. It is always upon these that heathenism places its heaviest blight. For the Garo village woman, life is a long day of labour with a short night of rest. They dry the rice and pound it to free it from the husk, they carry water from the stream and wood from the jungle, they cook, smear the floors with mud, gather silkworms from the jungle, feed them, spin and weave. In the garden-season the women transplant the young rice plants and help cut the ripened grain. Nevertheless, some of them have very sweet womanly faces,—such faces as the Gospel produces among all peoples.

There were many, many things that were new to me. I saw more of the Gospel's accomplishments in that one week than I had seen in the three years in Gauhati station. Those men led their meetings, elected their officers and conducted

their business along proper parliamentary lines.
. . . The sad part is that the men seem advanced
so far beyond the women that they cannot be com-
rades in many things.   Truly, it is only in Christ
Jesus that there is neither male nor female.   The
men are decently clothed, for the most part.   Often
they wear a coat or blanket in addition to their
shirt, and sometimes they have shoes and stockings; whereas the women usually have only a sack-
like garment coming from under the arms to mid-
way between the knees and ankles; at night they
wear cotton over the upper part of the body,
but very seldom a bodice or shirt, almost never a
coat, blanket or shawl, and never shoes and stockings.   While I shivered in my heavy coat in the
cold night-fogs, the women sitting all around me
took off the covering from their shoulders to wrap
it about some of their little children that slept at
their feet, leaving their own shoulders and bosom
exposed to the cold.

These same hard-worked, ill-dressed women
have paid very nearly fifty dollars to send eight
girls chosen from different churches of the district
to our boarding-school.   These people are so poor
that it is almost impossible for them to pay anything as individuals.   They will make more effort
to educate their boys, but they are not used to the
thought of educating a girl.   And Rhanji,—oh! I
love the honest, generous, loving heart under his
brown skin!   Rhanji gets sixteen rupees a month

and is going to keep four of his nieces in school, paying six rupees for their board and finding all their clothes, books, and supplies. Rhanji is an inspiring joy. As we were coming home with the girls, I walked behind Rhanji on the trail, and the dear, baby-loving bachelor confided to me these big thoughts, " You know, Missahib, these girls going into school mean more than we see today. They will go in and get things that are good to know; then they will come back and slowly, slowly, the village will have what the girls got in school; and another year more girls will go from other villages and they will get these things to share in their villages; and then it will be with us something as it is with the sahibs and memsahibs in the house." He meant, I think, that then Garo husbands and wives will share all things, even their thoughts, as missionary husbands and wives do.

Gauhati, Assam,
March 24, 1916.

Dear Little Mother:

. . . Last week there was a great Hindu festival on. I have always heard it spoken of as the red powder puja, because red powder is thrown on pedestrians much as flour used to be thrown by children at Hallowe'en at home. This is supposed to be the most obscene of Hindu festivals, one about which one is constantly warned not to ask questions. It is the principal festival of the year in the section in which our Hindu pundit lives. People of that region treasure their specially fine cloths, loom-parts, brassware, ivory and other produce to exhibit and sell at this time. I have long wanted to visit the pundit's home and so get an inside view of Hindu life, and this holiday was my last opportunity to do so before going home; so I went.

It was decided that I must have one of the servants go with me in case anything happened. The bearer was sent but missed the early morning train, so the pundit and I started off alone. And yet not alone, either, for every available inch of space in the whole train was taken before we left Gauhati. People were even crowded in the baggage car, a closed steel compartment without windows. It was a local train, and at every station along the way there were frantic scrambles for places—the people inside, screaming lest they be mashed in the jam, and beating back those on the outside who tried to force their way into the already overcrowded space. The guards shoved in passengers wherever they could get a footing.

We left the train at a little sun-baked station, supposedly five miles from the village. It was about half-past twelve and very, very hot. A young elephant and a pony were waiting at the station, and I was to take my choice of the animals. Need I say that I made the elephant kneel and make stepping stones of his various joints, up which I climbed by the aid of his howdah rope-banister. There was not the regular howdah sort of chair that royalty and Europeans usually use when traveling by elephant, but only a plain kind of small mattress tied on with rope. We went as the birds fly—over the rice fields—shadeless, hot and dusty, but with a strong breeze. That five miles was closely related to twenty! We stopped at a Hindu village about half-way. The people gathered from nap, field and rice-pounding to stare at me. The village leader refreshed me with milk from a green cocoanut pulled while I entertained the women with pictures of Satribari and of you folk at home. None of the women and but few of the men had ever seen a white woman before. All along the road, men and women in the different villages through which we passed, asked where I was going, why I had come, and was the pundit going to have me for another wife!

At the pundit's house everything was ready to receive me. Full-grown banana trees had been cut down and planted at the entrance of the court-yard, after the approved fashion of honouring a guest. I was to occupy the prayer-house. The building was unwalled, but half of it had been screened in with portable bamboo mats and furnished with a chair, two tables and a bed with planks for a mattress. Some fruit was in brass dishes on a newspaper tablecloth. From the time of my arrival, Saturday about dusk, until I left

Monday morning about nine or ten o'clock, I was a source of great interest to the men, women and children. They were very curious as to my dressing and undressing, my eating and sleeping. . . . They gathered in the morning before sunrise and separated the screens to see how I slept. I kept my eyes closed, pretending to sleep and hoping they would go away. When I turned over, this was reported by one of the watchers and others gathered to see if I would do it again. I happened to use the hand on which I wear my cameo ring to draw the covers closer over my face. This important action was reported to the waiting crowd.

Since my eating or cooking in any of their buildings would have hopelessly polluted the same, they had erected a little enclosure of banana-tree stalks, with two holes in the ground for cooking. . . . I knew that I would have fruit, so had brought only a bottle of malted milk and a tin of crackers, thinking these would suffice for the few days I intended to stay. Upon my arrival, a number of the leading men of the village were called together to decide whether or not I might be offered milk without endangering the caste of the villagers. After discussion it was decided that as I had come as a guest to the village, was thirsty and travelworn, the warm milk might be offered me. I drank it. It is always a trial to drink cow's milk here in India for the cows are so poorly fed that the milk tastes dirty, oily and altogether nasty.

ELLA MARIE HOLMES—

"One of those Foreign Missionaries"

In the evening my host came to me in great straits
to know what could be done about giving me food.
The bearer had missed the train and they could
not cook anything for me, but they would send
for a Mohammedan from a village a mile or more
away, for Mohammedans do not have caste, so
may cook for Christians. When I found out that
the villagers might boil water for me without hurt-
ing their caste, I assured them that with boiled
water I could make malted milk and would have
all that I desired and get along beautifully. . . .
The bearer arrived that evening.

In the evening the village headman, the priest,
surveyor, tax-collector, and another official came
to pay their respects and to see what I was like.
The priest is a young man studying in a Hindu
divinity school in Gauhati and home only for the
holiday. He spent the first part of the evening
gauging and weighing me. Evidently he decided
that he could risk the contamination of acquain-
tance and became quite cordial, asking me to see
his wife the next day. After the men left, the
women and children crowded in again and I entertained them until about ten o'clock when we all
went with the pundit's mother to see the fireworks.
It was about twenty minutes' walk. All the rice-
field paths were alive with others bent to the center field whither we were making our way. Being
women, we waited at every crossing until the front
path was clear of men,—this although all in our

party were very old women, women who served
and do not observe purdah, or little girls who had
not yet been kept in purdah.

We sat down under a great tree and after a
while torch-bearers came with singing and dancing carrying in their midst the gohain, or priestly
incarnation of God. The whole crowd sang, rock-
ets were fired, balloons were sent up, illuminations
and set pieces lighted. Apart from photographs
and elaborate set pieces, these fireworks compare
very favourably with those seen on Inauguration
Day and other notable occasions on the Monu-
ment grounds in Washington. I supposed they
had been purchased in Calcutta and was dumb-
founded to find that they had been made by the
villagers on the spot at a cost of about five hundred
rupees. One very striking phase of the celebra-
tion was the burning of a grass hut in which a
goat had been bound but allowed to escape if he
could as the hut blazed. I have not yet been able
to learn the significance of this custom.

I was tired, so about midnight asked to be ex-
cused and went home with the pundit's mother.
The latter and a little girl slept on the floor in my
room. I greatly alarmed the dear old lady when
I kneeled to pray. Evidently she thought I was
frightened or grieving and insisted upon my getting up from my knees!

. . . They had a jungle-fowl shot for my dinner
Sunday. They couldn't touch it, so the bearer

brought it in from the jungle where it had fallen. It would have been pollution to have brought it into their courtyard so I was called outside to see it. The bearer had to take it back to the jungle to clean it and leave it there all day. He cooked it in the little house of banana stalks and I had to go out there to eat it or the pundit would have had to burn down the other house.

Sunday I saw the village water-tank. It is green and foul. Everyone bathes in it when he comes to get his supply of water. There had been a scourge of smallpox in the village. More than a score of children bore the scars and on some the sores had not healed. A number had died with the disease, for there is no effort to segregate or vaccinate although the Government would have sent a government vaccinator to any village that needed it, had the people been willing to have him come. When I asked the two college men of the village why they had not insisted upon a vaccinator coming to them, they said that the women and ignorant people of the village would not consent to it for fear they might anger the goddess of smallpox and she send an awful scourge upon them! When I visited the women of the priest's household, he wanted to have tea made for me, but I had decided to suffer extreme thirst rather than drink the bath-water of smallpox patients, even if it were boiled. With a pebble under my tongue, I walked miles Sunday, in great heat across un-

shaded rice-fields, visiting women in I know not
how many courtyards, and talking with them until
my parched tongue could scarcely move in my
dried, feverish mouth. . . . At the home of the
pundit's wife, they had a feast for me. It was
laid on a handkerchief spread over a beautiful
chased brass tray. There was milk (probably not
boiled, so not to be tasted), a hard-boiled egg that
had been shelled and thumb impressions taken on
the white meat, puffed rice balls dipped in syrup,
some sugar candy dusty from the bazaar, and
some sugar cane cut into small pieces. I nibbled
a bit of the candy, but knew that I was too thirsty
and water too scarce to venture much sweet, even
had it been clean. I devoured every bit of the
sugar-cane and for the first time found its juice
refreshing. When we got back to the pundit's
house about dark, I sucked the juice from an over-
ripe native melon and devoured hot milk as though
it were nectar for the gods. The headman and
surveyor took me to the fair grounds where the
people were sacrificing to the idols. The Brahmins here said that if I took off my shoes I might
go up where they sat right in front of the idols,
provided I would make an offering to them. Need-
less to say, I contented myself with seeing them
from a distance. There were about ten drummers
and six cymbal-clangers dancing in front of the
idols. They were dripping with perspiration, although naked to the waist.

At night, after the men went back to the fair, I went out and sat down with the women at their evening prayers. They sing their prayers as they clap their hands, one acting as leader and the others answering her. It was altogether weird, and I was glad to steal off to bed even though later the women brought the lantern back and stood around looking at me.

Monday we walked across the rice-fields to the station in one of the densest dust-storms I've known. I was so parched with thirst that I had to stop by the road and send the men to one of the villages to buy green cocoanuts that I might drink the milk before I could go on. You see it was the end of the long dry season with a blustery March wind to blow the dust. . . . I'd not exchange this experience for a month or two of just ordinary living. . . .

After five-and-a-quarter years' service I went home on furlough, marveling at what God had wrought in spite of my failures and foolishness, and asking Him to allow me to go back again to try to do better. But I wanted to go back with my sister Nettie as self-supporting missionaries. So far as I know, in all of Assam all foreigners that are at all actively engaged in Christian service are paid workers. Several Hindus and Mohammedans have remarked to me that missionaries follow their vocation even as lawyers and physi-

cians follow theirs, viz., they make their living so;
that unsalaried Christian foreigners such as commercial men, officials, travelers, do not seem to be
burdened with Christian work. I have often wondered why more Christians of independent means
do not live in non-Christian lands as laymen active
in Christian service.

VI

ON FURLOUGH AND BACK TO WORK: MY SISTER NETTIE

PART of my furlough was spent in a business venture designed to finance my sister Nettie and myself on the field. After our business failed I had six weeks' experience in hospital training, and then was busy with deputation work. Possibly deputation work is the most trying part of a missionary's training. A healthy sense of humor is a helpful asset on the foreign field and just as helpful in deputation work. I think Christ sent His servants out two-by-two, knowing that two are better than one, not only because the one will lift up his fellow, but also that they might have someone with whom to laugh. Often what might appear mean or hard to a lone individual, will be an occasion for laughter when there is someone with whom to laugh.

There are, for instance, such things as being met at the station by the pastor of the church in which you are to speak, and have this man of four years' college and three years' seminary training, greet you with the query, " Are you the foreign missionary? " What a temptation to reply, " Yes, one of the species!"

Then there is the pleasure of having the one
who is to introduce you to your audience, ask
you, after you have gone on the platform, in what
mission field you have served, and the nature of
your work, then give an introduction something
like this: "We are indeed privileged today in
having Miss ——— with us. We have all read
about our sister's work in *Missions* and other
sources, and have followed her with interest, which
will be all the greater after having had her with
us today, and having looked into her face and
heard her tell personally about her work."

Every missionary who has done much deputation work finds it difficult to refrain from smiling
when, after a long, hard day of reports followed
by a luncheon and pageant, then more reports, and
after many have left on early trains and the rem-
nant is weary, the presiding officer announces:
"We have saved the best until the last" (sometimes it is, "saved the cream for the last"). "We
have with us one of our dear missionaries whom
we all delight to honour, and she will take these
last moments (usually seven to fifteen minutes)
to tell us about her work."

Securing entertainment is frequently another
source of amusement. As you stand, the center
of a group, Mrs. X says that she would so love
to have the missionary in her home, but Mr. X
is not very well. Mrs. Y would be so pleased to
take you home with her, but she is having some

painting done. Mrs. Z assures you that she would not let anyone else have the privilege of entertaining you, but would selfishly claim it for herself, had she not two small children who make more noise than would be good for a tired speaker. Mrs. X suggests that Mrs. B be asked to take you—" she is always willing to put people up, and has such a nice home." Mrs. B graciously accepts the guest offered her and proves a most delightful hostess with a family well-trained in the somewhat neglected art of true hospitality. This condition is usually limited to city churches. In rural districts one is apt to suffer from excessive entertainment, sometimes having three successive meals in the same town, with three different families, the missionary entertaining the company invited for each meal, while the hostess is busy in the kitchen.

Not yet has my bump of humor developed sufficiently to enable me to be amused or to smile when the matter of my expenses is being discussed in front of me, and two women hand me each a dollar bill, while the third fishes in her purse for two dimes and three nickels, which she hands me for " your work." But I can greet with a grin a written request from a prominent mission worker to spend three extra days away from home (directly after two weeks of constant, hard deputation work and entertainment in thirteen strange homes) so as to fill two engagements in the same town but four days apart, on one railroad ticket and so save the " large Young People's division " of a wealthy city church three dollars car-fare. I wanted to reply that I had not found anyone in California willing to do any kind of work or waiting for one dollar a day. P. W. Wilson's *The Christ We Forget,* in the third chapter, under " A Mother's Influence," has a pertinent paragraph that we might take to heart with profit: " Jesus was brought up as a gentleman, considerate of others, yet able to rebuke all liberties. Simon the Pharisee might be rich, and our Lord longed to win his heart; but Simon must not forget the usual courtesies of a host, merely because Jesus was a missionary without private means."

There is the other side of deputation work, too. There are the Bethany homes into which the missionary is taken as one of the family, where she finds rest and refreshment of body, enjoys spiritual quickening and fellowship and adds to those friendships that last through the years, and enrich life with memories of happy homes. I think no missionary would wish to escape the embarrassments due to such lack of courtesy as has been previously noted, if such escape should entail the foregoing of the blessings found in Bethany homes. I have cited some of the embarrassments, believing that they arise, generally, from thoughtlessness and hoping that to mention them may add to the Bethany type of hospitality and courtesy.

When in September, 1917, my sister Nettie and I sailed together for India, the dream of years was fulfilled, the desire of our heart gratified, and our cup of happiness full and overflowing. The years of our separation made us appreciate more perfectly the gracious Providence that now assigned us to the same field of service. With Nettie at hand to inspire and hold me to my best, I felt able to do and endure anything that the years might bring. So I plunged into a new term of service resolved, under God, that it should be free from the mistakes that had marred my first term.

The inauguration of a Language School, where our new missionaries might study the vernacular under more favourable circumstances than had heretofore been enjoyed, getting hold again of the cottages and class-room work, and training teachers, soon dragged me into the old rut of incessant work.

Then influenza came to India, exacting a toll of 2,000,000 lives in about six months. On our school compounds fifty-three girls, teachers and servants were laid low. There was no doctor, no nurse. We bought pound bottles of bicarbonate of soda and salicylate of soda, which Nettie helped to weigh, mix and wrap the powders. None of our patients were lost and only one developed pneumonia, although most of them ran a temperature of 104° and over. In the midst of the scourge, I noticed Nettie's bright eyes and florid cheeks, so took her temperature and sent her to bed with fever of 102.6°. For some time before Nettie had been troubled with a cough which the doctors attributed to acclimation. There was so much to be done that Nettie got up before she should have. The cough persisted and strength did not return. This was at Christmas, 1918.

The following letters I wrote to my sister Bertha, in the ensuing year:

Eden Bari, Mongaldai, Assam,
19th January, 1919.

Dear Bertha:
From " Satribari," you know that " bari " means garden, so you may gather from the above that I am in the Garden of Eden! It is a village of Kacharis on the north bank of the Brahmaputra River, and has been Christian for about four years. The men seem to be unusually earnest in matters of religion and of good calibre generally. The women are in comparison with their men on about a par with the Garo women as compared with Garo men. . . .

I have just come from church. There were about eighty or one hundred present. . . . The only woman who could read was one of their girls who came with me from the boarding school. . . . The men assemble quietly and sit reverently during the entire service. But in the middle of a hymn the women come up to shake hands with me and present a couple of eggs. Throughout the service they come and go, talk to one another and scold their children, just as they please. . . . The women have had no leader or helper, and how sadly they need one. We came over here to see about buying the year's supply of rice for the boarding school, and I came also to spy out the land, because after this year I am hoping to be able to leave school-work and do evangelistic work. So I want to see what the fields and needs are. I wish that it were the beginning of my first term rather than my second and that I had the Kachari as well as the Assamese language, and several lives to live instead of one. I don't know yet just how a missionary could get hold of these women to help them, but there must be a way since there is such a crying need. The women and children are so poorly dressed, so untidy and filthy, so poor and aged for their years. The mother of one of my girls looks as old as an octogenarian, and yet she has a daughter only about eleven and the pastor says that she is " a very old woman, about forty-five or fifty!" So I suppose she isn't nearly as old as she is aged.

In spite of what they lack, there is a great difference between these Christian Kacharis and their non-Christian neighbours. . . . Just now they are harvesting their rice. This morning when the church bell rang and we walked to

church we passed the people from neighbouring
heathen villages, some bringing in sheaves, some
cutting in the fields and others driving oxen to
tread out the grain. I realized then as I never had
before that observing the Sabbath is hard for these
poor farmers in the harvest season when every
day's labour counts for so much and no extra
help is procurable. . . .

I am staying in the preacher's house. . . . There
are some twenty people in his establishment with
a dozen or so houses for his family, help, office,
grain and cattle. . . . I am occupying the office.
. . . There is a bed of four good planks on legs,
a table with a red oilcloth full of pictures. There
are two good chairs and a bench in the room, beside another bed made out of empty Singer sewing machine boxes. Under this bed they must
have put all the rubbish from under the bed prepared for me, for my bed is clean underneath, but
the Singer sewing machine bed looks like a rag and
old clothes' picker's cart. . . . Just now they have
brought in my morning rice in a beautiful chased
bellmetal dish, water in a bright brass lota, and a
brass basin in which to wash my hands. . . .
Getting a bath has been the greatest difficulty.
They watch me so all day, particularly the children, even opening the door when I have shut it,
and peeping in through the bamboo windows. So
last night when I knew that all the men and boys
were in a meeting and the women and girls were

asleep, I went out to the little mountain stream that flows beside the house, and had a bath in my kimono just at midnight, getting so cold through to the marrow of my bones that I didn't get warm enough to go to sleep the rest of the night. . . .

Different villagers bring us chickens, fruit and eggs, saying that they have neither table, chair nor brass vessels in their poor homes and that they do not know how to cook curry for a European to eat, but they want to entertain us, so send these things to the preacher's house.

. . . Nettie's cold is still bad. Just before we came here, I called the civil surgeon in to examine her. He found nothing wrong, but prescribed rest, cod-liver oil, a tonic and something with which to rub her chest and back. He thought she would be well in four or five days. . . . Dr. Crozier is going to pass through next week on his way to meet Mrs. Crozier. I'm writing him today asking him to stop over a day and give Nettie a thorough examination. . . . The phase that I do not like is a frequent rise in temperature towards evening, but some evenings she is normal, so I hope the temperature may be malaria. . . .

16th March, 1919.

Dear Father:

. . . We've made quite a number of acquisitions to our household during the last fortnight. First came a cow and her calf. The cow gives a quart of milk a day, and sometimes less; usually less since we have had her, although the man from whom we bought her assured us that it would usually be more. We want to get a couple more cows now, so as to be supplied with sufficient milk for our babies. . . . We've also bought a cart and pair of oxen. But the most exciting purchase of all is a pony. . . . He's destined for Eden Bari, the villages thereabout and for the Garo villages in our district, when I am released for evangelistic work. I paid only sixty rupees for him and five rupees to the coachman for driving the bargain. He is from Manipur, the original home of polo. . . . Up to the time we purchased him, he is supposed never to have been fed or watered but to have depended upon his own efforts to get food from the jungle. Neither had he been shod or clipped. He was as nervous and frightened at a bucket as he could possibly have been at a loaded motor-truck; he was shy of my hand, as suspicious of his first taste of grain and as tremblingly timid about eating from a box, as the worst country codger could be at the most elaborately laid banquet table in a princely banquet-hall. But he hasn't been long getting used to the ways of civilization. He stood having his hair cut very well until they tried to clip under his head and about his feet. He must have thought that therein lay the source of his strength, for he did the most wonderful feats of feet, whenever they diplomatically approached any of his extremities with the shears. . . .

. . . Nettie's cough seems a little better. . . .

April 5, 1919.

. . . About ten days ago we had a death in the boarding department. It was Anoograu, the little baby we took from the hospital when her mother died of pneumonia. I think I wrote you that she had fits and a skin disease when we first took her. Her head was one great scab, and her hands and arms became so covered with ulcerated sores that we had to keep them in bags. And yet, she was always so good, so happy and bewitching that everybody loved her. The fits became less and less frequent. . . . She was having a hard time teething, so I took her to the Government hospital Monday and had her gums cut. She seemed better, only rather drowsy, and Wednesday morning the matron called me to see the child and I found her in a state of coma. I sent for the doctor immediately and we worked over her until she came. . . . She lifted the baby from her cradle on the floor to a high bed and the heart stopped while the child was being lifted. We banked a box with beautiful blossoms very like our lilacs only with lacey leaves, and we put the little form in the mass of blossoms. She looked as though she had fallen asleep in a garden. . . . The little thing evidently had a sad heritage, so it may be well that she slipped away as she did, but she was one of the dearest babies I have known, of any colour whatsoever. . . . It is the first baby I've lost; for the little tea-garden baby we had we took to bury, really, for we knew that it was dying when we received it.

Just now I am keeping Birsi, the little Lakimpur baby, in my room. She has had dysentery several times. I would keep her in my room until she seemed cured, then send her back to the dormitory, when the disease would develop again. As the child is only a skeleton with an enormous spleen from constant fever, I don't dare run any risks with her. Then, too, we think she has kalazhar, which is very contagious, so we want to safeguard the other babies. In the bungalow she has become a new child: happy, chatty, and playful. Before she had smiles for no one and the girls thought her a dunce. When I am working at my desk or about my bedroom I keep her on a cushion in a big chair and talk mother's nonsense with her as I have time. She talks back and gurgles with joy and excitement. Just now as I write, she is sleeping soundly on my lap. This is the part of the work that I love and for which I know I have gifts and skill, but the part for which I have to steal time from school work. . . . The missionaries are convinced that I was born to teach school. . . . I'd rather look after a half-dozen babies and sick folk and help them to live, to love

to live and to help other folk to love to live, than
I would to be the most successful teacher of the
largest school in India. But then, that is nothing
to bother you with.

Nettie's cough is bad again. I'm begging her
to go down to Calcutta next week with Mr. and
Mrs. Stephen and enter a hospital where she can
be under constant watch care and have someone
find out just where this cough is seated and how
to unseat it. . . .

> Calcutta,
> Sunday (I think it's the
> 5th of May), 1919.

My Dear Family:

I wonder if within this generation means of
communication will become so perfected that sitting here in Calcutta I may speak with you in
Washington. . . . There is much that I would
like to talk about tonight—things I'd like to dis-
cuss. But since discussion is out of the question,
I can only ask the Great Father to give needed
guidance and wisdom, believing that you, too, will
be asking this same blessing for us and so through
prayer we may be drawn closer together.

You'll probably be surprised to see this letter
dated Calcutta. Last Saturday I had a letter from
Mrs. Stephen to the effect that Nettie was having
a daily temperature of 101°, was losing weight,
and evidently longing to get home, since she knew

that she must go. . . . I decided immediately to
leave on the mail train Monday. . . . I am more
than glad that I came since everybody seems to
think that Nettie is much brighter. And I have
been able to secure sailings for both of us on the
Santa Cruz, a Pacific Mail steamer, due to sail
from Calcutta direct to San Francisco the 20th
of May.

From my last letter you will know that Nettie
has tuberculosis. I had hoped that it might still
be incipient, but it has advanced beyond the first
stage. . . . I wish we might be getting away long
before the twentieth, but we are really very fortunate to have secured passage via the Pacific even
as early as this. . . . At first they could give us
no berths and no hopes of securing berths, but I
would not take " No " for an answer. Every time
I came away from the hospital it was with the conviction that we *must* get away on this steamer.
When I came home from the hospital Friday night
Mr. Stephen brought me a huge pile of mail and
said he thought I would like to glance through
them as one seemed to be from the steamer company. And so it was—promising us two berths!

. . . Nettie is down to eighty-three pounds.
She has no pain but a daily temperature and is
very weak. I wanted to take her for a drive and
thought taking her to have her passport pictures
taken was a splendid excuse for getting her away.
But the Sister wouldn't hear of her going out in

"SISTER NETTIE"—

On the eve of sailing for Assam

a carriage, or in fact, of her going out in any way. She said that Nettie was far too weak for such excursions. . . . I'll be glad when she becomes my patient. The Sister is very nice to her, and so in fact everybody is,—they can't help but be, for Nettie is such an appreciative patient, but it is a big ward and there are many to care for, so none can have all done for them that an individual nurse would do for a single patient. Since coming down here, I've again begged Nettie to go into a private room, but she won't listen to it; she says she much prefers staying out on the veranda. She is brave and happy, as all who know her, would expect her to be. . . . Everybody has been unspeakably kind. I'm sure we have had a hundred letters in the last ten days or so, with loving offers of service and expressions of sympathy and encouragement. . . . Recently I have been hearing of wonderful T. B. cures which have been effected out West and I am hoping that Nettie's case will be another wonderful cure that people may soon be citing to others upon whom the dread disease has a hold. . . . I am confident that Nettie is not worrying about herself at all—her mind and heart are too full of all the beautiful things with which she has been enriching them these many years. And I cannot, I will not, consider anything but a complete recovery for her. Too many little children need her loving motherly training, sincerity and

simplicity; and my impetuosity needs the balance
of her sensible sanity. It is true, she is quite fit
to be called up higher, but I believe God will let
her stay yet a while longer with us, that we may
share her fitness.

25th May, 1919.

Dear Home-folk:

You see we are really started and all promises
well for Nettie. . . . The wonderful providences
that have marked all our way, still attend us. . . .
Nettie's nurse is engaged to one of the river pilots.
He arranged for Nettie to get on board the
steamer at one-thirty today, before anyone else
was around and early enough to be well rested before her medical exam. Then the two young
Americans in the passenger office wrote the Purser,
asking that Nettie be vouchsafed every possible
comfort. . . . There is a very nice Stewardess on
board. We have been put just opposite the ladies'
bath and near the ship's doctor. . . . There is a
nice lot of passengers on board. . . . It is good to
look out and see Old Glory flying in the breeze.
. . . Nettie wants me to tell you how fine she is
and how full of promise everything is. And just
now things do seem more promising than they
have for weeks. Nettie lost a pound and a half
last week, but I suppose everybody in Calcutta
lost this much in the heat. Do not worry about

her. . . . The pilot will carry this back to Calcutta to mail. . . .

It was too late to avert disaster. For more than
a week on the voyage home we were prepared to
bury Nettie at sea. But an indomitable will rallied
fagging strength so that she was able, with assist-
ance, to walk from the steamer to the dock when
we reached San Francisco. For more than a year
Nettie suffered, glorified God, and with increased
power supplemented the lessons of faith and love
that through the years she had been teaching her
sister-friend.

Her going away is one of the dark mysteries,
for light upon which we must wait " until the day-
break and the shadows flee away."   In her short
term of service in India, she had made herself very
useful and greatly loved.   Scholars and servants
alike testified that her use of Assamese was more
idiomatic and perfect in the ears of the Assamese,
than had been acquired by any other European
except Mr. Moore. This achievement is the more
remarkable in view of the fact that Nettie had
received no linguistic training and was thirty-one
years old when she began her language work.   It
may be partly accounted for by the fact that her
mentality was above the average and because she
put hours of concentrated study upon the language. Since some others have spent more hours
with not as good results, I am inclined to attribute

Nettie's success in language work more to the fact that, conscious of her lack of training for such study, she very definitely depended upon God's help and worked prayerfully with her books and pundits.

She was peculiarly a chosen vessel of honor, sanctified and meet for the Master's use; she seemed not to need the purging of suffering. European and character-discerning Indian alike, were impressed with her innate goodness. One would have supposed her destined for long years of service in the place of great need to which she had been sent. Why, then, was she given but a year and a half? And why did she have to supplement this with more than a year of suffering? Since her going away I have thought much about these things. Inasmuch as with the Lord one of her days of perfect service may be as a thousand years, she may have served longer than we ken. And her suffering?

*"We suffer. Why we suffer,—that is hid
With God's foreknowledge in the clouds of heaven."*

She was content " to set ' her ' soul to suffer perfectly " and not to question " why." Never once in all those months, so far as I know, did her faith falter. In no part of her life was she a greater blessing than in those last months of her suffering.

Surely in some way impossible of our understanding here and now, God must, in the taking of such souls to Himself, be exercising the same divine love and wisdom, the same matchless economy, that all His revealed dealings proclaim.

After Nettie went Home, God allowed me some training in the school of trial and perplexity. I found myself drawn into the intimacies of heart-and-home secrets of others. I battled anew with the mystery of sorrow, disappointment and tragedy. I saw the principles of Jesus Christ applied to broken hearts and lives, result in their healing; I witnessed Christ's precepts of love and forgiveness speak peace to domestic storms and repair the havoc of home tragedies; I watched men and women who had suffered the loss of that which in the secret, sacred places of the heart they most cherished, come up from the valley of the shadows of sorrow with peace marked on the battle-ground of their faces, as they went forth forgetting self in serving others. Pain and sorrow are still mysteries, but I know that Christ sheds a light upon them that brings strength out of struggle, and peace out of storm. I know, also, that this light in the darkness, has come and can come from no other source than Christ.

It was then that I saw the mud walls of Indian huts crumble away and within I saw my brown friends without God and without hope in the world, blind and in Christless darkness, grope for light as they, too, lifted empty arms while the hungry heart cried, " Where? " and the weary mind asked

" Why? " Mocked by disappointed hopes, and
tragic denials, I saw other brown friends question
why it had to be and ask how they could go on
after defeat. So with a more sympathetic com-
passion for India's unshepherded sheep and a more
understanding love, I sailed the third time for
Assam, to help Christ " give light to them that sit
in darkness, and in the shadow of death, to guide
their feet into the way of peace."

VII

CARRYING ON

IT was in February, 1914, that I had my first trip out into the district, forty to sixty miles from Gauhati, where our Christian villages are hidden in bamboo clumps beside rivers. All the three days' journey back from the jungle to the station, I was building a little " house by the side of the road " somewhere in the district near a bazaar center, planting gardens around it and peopling it with throngs of sick brown people coming for medicines, ignorant ones coming for books and learning, mothers coming with babies to learn how best to nourish and care for them, and sinning, sorrowing men and women coming to find the Saviour. All the years I spent in school-work were hounded by the vision of this house by the side of the road, and every trip to the jungle afforded new details for the dream house and the work to be done by it.

Friends and different organizations in my home church gave me a purse of five hundred dollars before I returned to Assam, and this helped interpret the dream into reality. While seeking out a location for the camp-house, I did evangelistic work in and around Gauhati, and helped put into shape

the second year's course of language study for new
missionaries.   In February, I attended the Kam-
rup Garo Christian Association and wrote the following letters to my Mother and the folks at home:

Gauhati, Assam, India,
Feb., 1922.

Dear Mother-mine:

. . . I want to warn you not to be concerned
if you do not get mail from me very regularly
these next few months.   Sometimes I will not be
within reach of a post-office when the weekly mail
goes out.   Sometimes I'll be on the north bank,
and sometimes up in the hills on this side of the
river. . . . Neither be worried because of anything you may chance to see in the papers.   Things
have been somewhat disturbed around Assam, but
we all believe that the situation is much better
than it was and are confident that the British
Government can handle it.   In accordance with
Gandhi's gospel of non-coöperation, the people
hereabouts refused to pay taxes and looted carts,
ostensibly to confiscate and destroy any foreign
goods they might be conveying.   So the Government had to send an officer with several hundred
sepoys to collect taxes.   The soldiers are stationed
at Boko, the people are paying their taxes and
" swaraj " seems as unattainable today as it was
several years ago when Gandhi inaugurated his
crusade and slogan. . . .

Personally, I feel perfectly safe and wondrously happy—happy as I imagine birds are when on the wing. I am positive that I am in God's place for me and am expecting His blessing on the work out here in the district. Let me tell you of an experience of His wonderful answer to prayer. Thursday I walked ten miles with the girls in the hottest part of the day on a dusty, shadeless road. Then the motor car that had carried the rest on, came back and picked us up for the next twenty-five miles or so. It had engine trouble, so we were delayed. It was dusk when we reached the end of the road where we had to leave the motor and walk the last five miles through a jungle. This jungle is a forest reserve and is so dense that it is dusk even in daylight. So it was very dark shortly after we entered it. There was a good moon that pierced the dark with darts of light. Much of the way a mountain stream was the only path, so there was nothing to do but take off shoes and stockings and splash in the water. It was gratefully cold to our tired feet, but oh, the stones and pebbles! The girls didn't mind them at all for they are always barefooted and the soles of their feet are like leather. After about a mile of this sort of travel, we came out upon an open space and after a bit were fronted with two paths. The two girls who were most familiar with that section decided that the upper path was the right one. We followed it some distance when again we

were confronted with two paths. By this time the
girls admitted that they didn't know the way. It
was about seven-thirty. We had been on the road
twelve hours and had eaten nothing since early
morning. So the girls were beginning to get
panicky,—and no wonder, for they knew that
about three weeks before, while burning the jungle
just a mile or two away, two men had been killed
by a tiger.

Then we remembered " from whence cometh our
help," so knelt there on the hill and asked God to
direct our path. While we were yet rising from
our knees the sharp report of a gun came along
the direction of the lower path. We knew that
the gun had been shot in the village for which we
were bound, for every evening of the Association
they give this sign when about to close the Association storehouse. So does God hear and answer
prayer. Singing "He Leadeth Me," and "What
a Wonderful Saviour," we retraced our steps and
were soon in camp. With such a God to care for
us, surely we have no need to fear one for the
other. . . .

On the north bank of the Brahmaputra River
was a new Christian community of Kacharis, num-
bering nearly one thousand. The women had become Christians because the men of their household had adopted the new faith, but they had only
a negative knowledge of the religion they pro-

fessed. They knew that Christians are supposed not to beat their wives and are not allowed more than one wife; they are not allowed to worship idols; they must not make or drink beer, toddy, or other intoxicants, and are not permitted to work or to buy and sell on Sunday. Around their negative concept of Christianity had gradually grown up ideas of schools and books, church and hymnals, more clothing (particularly shoes), and the substitution of repeated awkward handshakes for their own graceful salaam, as a greeting. None of the mothers could read or write, and knew little or nothing of the doctrine they were supposed to adorn. During the five years that their own field-missionary had been in America, this great group of earnest, ignorant young Christians had but one or two brief visits annually from a missionary from another field and no work had been undertaken for the women.

In the midst of this community there was a village that in its non-Christian state had been known as " Gahorigaon," or " The Village of Swine," because of the numbers of hogs that wallowed in mire around most of the mud houses. After becoming Christians, the men of Gahorigaon wanted a new name for their village. They went to their Bibles and read about a garden that the Lord God planted, where grew every tree that is pleasant to the sight, and good for food, and a river went out to water the garden. It seemed a description of their own village minus the hogs, so they did away with the swine, built a church for the tree of life and a school for the tree of knowledge, and called their village " Edenbari,"—" bari " meaning garden.

After I had planned to build my house by the side of the road in this Garden of Eden, word was received that the missionary who had previously worked the field was returning shortly, but without his wife, who was staying in the States with their little girl. So it would have been unwise for a single woman to live in the same community, hence the house had to be located on the south bank of the Brahmaputra River. After several other sites had been selected and for one and another reason had to be given up, upon the advice of a government official the house by the side of the road was finally located at Hahim Depot, at the foot of the Khasi Hills.

> *On the Train Going to Jorhat,*
> *Feb. 18, 1922.*

Where shall I begin? There is so much to write that the end will not be for some pages. . . . That was a happy, happy week in camp. I walked about fifty-five miles and some of it in the heat of the day, and seem none the worse for the exercise, so you may know that I am in excellent physical trim.

The Association closed Sunday night. . . . After we reached the second rest-house, coming back to

Gauhati, Isabella* and I went out to speak to some
children and distribute picture-cards amongst them.
As usual out in the district, the children were
afraid to receive them at first but after one ven-
turesome spirit dared to take the card into her
hand, little ones sprang up from hedges, houses
and ditches, and mothers came asking for cards for
absent children. We went to bed early, setting the
alarm for twenty minutes of four and leaving tea
in the thermos bottles for a bit of breakfast before
starting out in the morning. We slept together on
a wee single bed, so as to use some of our blankets
for a mattress over the metal springs. The next
morning we . . . started from the rest-house at a
quarter of five—the moonlight very bright and the
morning stars shining as brightly as the nearly full
moon would let them. Rhonji had to stay back
with the baggage to wait for the ox-cart that was
to come out from Gauhati. . . . So I slung a
thermos bottle of malted milk across one shoulder
and carried my topi-strap slung on the other arm
with the topi hanging down and making a pocket
for my revolver which had all six chambers loaded
in case we should meet with something along the
road. The air was fresh and chilly. We had
twelve miles to walk before quarter of nine, in
order to catch the public motor car that runs from
Palishbari to Gauhati. At first it was difficult to
read the numbers on the mile stones, but after

* Miss Wilson, my Gauhati colleague.

dawn we found that we did three miles an hour steadily. . . .

The morning we got into Gauhati, Mr. Stephen called to say that the Jungakoli bungalow which we hoped to buy from the Forest Department for my camp-house, is not for sale now. I felt he must have made a mistake for the place seems so ideal for our purpose that I thought it had to be mine. When I recovered from the shock of surprise, I clung desperately to the faith that God had something better in store, although I couldn't see what could be better. When the Forest Officer heard that I wanted one room for medicines and sick folks, he told Mr. Stephen to bring me along to have a talk with him. We went that afternoon and he said that if my little house was to be part hospital or dispensary, he was quite sure he could get me a grant of land and timber! Of course the words " hospital and dispensary " took my breath away and I hastened to explain that I was not qualified to run a hospital or dispensary but planned to stock simple remedies for fever, dysentery, running sores, sore eyes, etc., and to have two cots for some sick women or children that might be in need of a little careful nursing. I was told, however, that the experience I have had with the school children has probably qualified me better than I think. It seems the Government wants to establish little dispensaries around through the isolated villages, but cannot afford to do so. They particularly want me to give Kalazhar treatments. This is a wasting fever very much like T. B. It has decimated whole sections of Assam and caused the people to abandon numbers of villages. The theory is that the germ is carried by bedbugs. The disease is being successfully treated by venous injections. . . . It is saving many lives.

I plan to have Scripture texts painted on the dispensary walls and pictures of Christ as the great Physician and Comforter. We'll have a little Gospel talk and hymn every day. The Tuttles think it a wonderful opportunity and so do the others. . . . When I went to advise with Mr. and Mrs. Tuttle, they gave me the wonderful news that a cable had just come from home, "Five hundred dollars gold for Holmes at present rate of exchange." I'm sure that you sent it. So wonderfully, wonderfully, does God time His provisions according to our need. . . . Who but God could have done this? For a lack of additional funds for the house seemed to be the chief drawback to this new plan, but I told Ethel that if we really needed more money, God would send it down from above or in from around, or up from below, but it would be here when needed. And here it is! And here I raise another Ebenezer! You can imagine with what joy and gratitude and reverence I went back into the district with Augusta the next day to spy out the land. It is beautifully situated, of which more later. Two Christian households have set-

tled in the village. The wife in one house is one
of our old girls, Mohini. There are a considerable
number of Nepalese in the village, and within a
few miles there are dozens of villages of Garos,
Rabhas, Kacharis, etc., who have never heard the
Gospel. And there are populous Assamese villages
within easy reach by motor, where Christ has
never been lifted up. So the place seems a good
working base.

March 19, 1922.

Dear Home-folk:

I took twelve exposures of a Premo pack to help
you visualize in what a very pleasant place the
lines are fallen unto me and amongst what an interesting lot of folks I am to live. And here the
whole pack of films melted! So I'll have to do the
best I can with some word sketches.

Hahim is beautifully situated. The morning
sun creeps up over low wooded hills and drops at
night between two ranges of higher hills. I call
these western hills my letter-box, because in the
evening Sol is a postman charged with loving mes-
sages for you at home. The western hills are
beautiful with great clumps of bamboos like friends
waving plumed hats in greeting. At night the Little Bear dips his tail into the valley between two
ranges and the southern stars saddle higher hills
closer. From these southern hills a mountain stream
of considerable force winds a serpentine course

around the west and is lost in the valley where the tail of the Little Bear dips low. The evening skies are very beautiful here just now at the end of the long dry season. My neighbours have grouped these stars in an order handed down from long generations of forefathers who spent many nights every harvest in their little shelters in tree tops, keeping watch with the stars over their crops and guarding them from the ravages of wild beasts. The other night I pointed out different constellations and most of the boys and girls seemed familiar with their Garo names and the Garo fables behind the names.

After the long, dry season everything is parched and brittle. The ground rustles with fallen leaves, the fields and hillsides are brown with parched growth and black with the cinders of burnt jungle. The river has shrivelled into a harmless stream, scarcely waist-deep, with wide stretches of rocks and sand on its naked beaches. It is about two o'clock as I write, and the third week in March, but the heat is the heat of midsummer. Our little pup is panting in the shade on the cool, mud floor by the open door; the chickens are standing in the shade with open mouths, gasping for breath. I doubt if even a " big, fat, woolly one " would tempt them to run even a short distance in this sun. They have been burning jungle all about us; the air is heavy with smoke; bits of burned leaf are falling everywhere; we can hear the sharp report

of bursting bamboo and occasionally the roar of
consuming fire. In another three months the picture will be quite different. Then the earth will
be clothed in soft, rich greens and the rocks and
sand of the riverside will be buried in a strong,
swift current that will flood the lowlands, sing the
song of rushing waters night and day, and raise a
gulf between the peoples on its two banks. . . .

I often change my mind about the most fascinating children, because so many are fascinating. I
have almost decided definitely, however, that
Nepali children are the cream of winsomeness.
They are so spontaneous, have the sweetest piping
baby voices, and the longest, most grown-up style
of clothes. I took the picture of a little Nepali boy
and girl for you. These little ones are not Christians, but were at Sunday school last Sunday and
we became friends. The next day when I hunted
them down for their pictures the mother of the
little girl yanked her away and insisted upon dressing her proudly in all her best things and in some
of the mother's best things, too. Little girls wear
shawls over their heads, little basque waists, and
skirts that just escape the ground. So they look
for all the world like little old women or as though
they were playing dress-up. This girlie had a
green-and-red silk shawl, a red-and-pink basque
with a big necklace of silver coins outside it, and
a voluminous skirt of yellow flowers on a brown
background. She had bangles and anklets and ear-

rings and a nose-ring. The little boy wore flowing trousers down to his ankles and over it a white
shirt with a long, long tail hanging outside. Add
round baby faces with large brown eyes, heavy
black lashes, skin of soft tan, chubby baby hands
and feet, and even then you won't begin to have
an idea how fetching the youngsters are until you
have fallen under the spell of their baby voices.

These Nepalese used to work in a corundum
mine twenty miles back in the hills, but the mine
has been abandoned. Now the men gamble with
cards all day and most of the night, except when
they are quarrelling over the cards. Some of the
women keep little shops, for this is a big market
center. . . . People come from twenty miles back
in the hills to buy and sell here. They begin to
arrive Sunday at sunset. The Khasas with their
goods carried in a basket-chair peculiar to their
tribe; the women usually very heavily dressed, the
men often wearing just a loin curtain. Garos come
with their wares in another kind of basket.
Amongst non-Christian Garos, men and women
both are generally scantily clad. . . . And there
are the Nepalese with yards and yards of cloth in
the women's skirts and the men with pajamas to
the ankles. They camp in the open fields and on
the banks of the river, always with a fire. . . .

Monday morning the bazaar opens under little
thatch roofs beneath which the people sit on the
ground with their wares around them—betel-nuts,

rice, potatoes, onions, fish, salt, spices, candy, oil,
notions, cloth, soap, pottery and cattle. Most of
the small produce is arranged in little pice piles.
A pice is half-a-cent. All day the crowd changes.
Some stay for the two days; some sell their goods
and return home Monday. New people arrive
Monday afternoon and the bazaar sits again Tuesday until afternoon. These two days are our
harvest days. We play the graphophone and use
the magic lantern. Sometimes we have an audience of several hundred out under the stars. They
are very fond of the laughing songs and of the
American Indian songs with drums. We always
close with a hymn; very often it is, " Joy to the
World " or " Nearer My God, to Thee." Then
we tell them the old story of Jesus having come
to save us from our sins and crown our lives with
peace and joy.

Already we have had a number of calls to care
for ulcers and sores, and oh, the babies and children that are burning with fever and have skeleton
bodies and huge spleens! So many, many women
say, " This is the only child I have left; the others
have died of fever." And other women of wistful
face say, " I had sons and daughters, but they all
died." Some of the men told me that they consider
themselves very fortunate if they are able to raise
half of their children to reach their teens. I know
that there are many, many needs that I will not be
able to meet, but I know, too, that there are many

ways in which I can help save babies for their mothers and some souls for their Saviour. Since you know how I love nursing you will not wonder that I am glad to be here. . . .

"Nengtakram," the Garo name for my home, means "Rest-Haven." That is what I want it to become for many weary ones. Pray that God may bless my contact with these people to His glory and their salvation. . . .

For two months I lived in a wee shack without windows, but with a foot or two of open space between the four or five feet high walls and the low roof of rotten thatch, finished with ancient cobwebs and slits through which sunshine percolated and stars winked. The hut had once been used as a cook-shed and the smoke of many fires had burnished the bamboo of the frame-work into rich shades of copper and brown.

> *Nengtakram,*
> *Hahim Depot,*
> *Boko Post Office,*
> *Kamrup District,*
> *Assam,*
> *India.*
> *March 12, 1922.*

Dear Jack:

Haven't I an aspiring address? If you could see the house I am occupying you would see the necessity for an elaborate identification. It is in the village where I hope to have my bungalow, but for the present I am occupying a shelter that was used first as a storeroom and later as a chicken-house. The rats shared it when it was used as a granary, leaving tunnels in the dirt floor. These we have filled in and smeared with mud, so it is nice as a carpet except that it is still wet. The chickens resent our taking possession. We just moved in yesterday afternoon and one old hen insisted upon coming to her old haunt to lay an egg and all the chickens were determined to roost here. When we wouldn't let them in through the door, one by one, they tried to " climb up some other way." And they succeeded, too, for it is no feat for them to fly over four feet of reed wall through the two feet of open space above. . . .

You would have enjoyed being in camp with us last week on the north side of the Brahmaputra, for the place is a net-work of mountain streams and fishing is good. The people fish so much with so many different kinds of apparati, that one wonders that any fish are left. . . . You will be interested in the crudest, least sportsman-like method of fishing that I saw yesterday. . . . We walked to a village about a mile from here and were told that all the men were fishing, so went down to the river. They call this particular form of fishing, " gun fishing." They prepare an explosive, using sulphur mostly, I believe. They bind it in bark

THE DAILY BATH AND LAUNDRY, SATRIBARI

OX-CART AND DRIVER

and strips of banana-stalks, then throw it with great force into the water where they have located a goodly number of fish. The force of compact with the water produces an explosion. The fish are maimed and the men catch them as they flap about in the water. Yesterday they had about a bushel of fish in their basket. . . .

This afternoon we called on a Bengali gentleman and his household. He has two hooloos, a kind of monkey peculiar to Assam, I understand. They are black except for a ridge of white over the brow. As they have no tails, they use their arms for climbing, so have developed them to a remarkable length. They have a passionate fondness for men. They are quite tame, whine after their master, follow him about as puppies do, and cling to him as babies to their mothers. . . . I'm sure you would want one if you could have seen these this afternoon. . . .

This is bazaar day. . . . A great medley of folk are in from miles and miles back in the hills carrying their wares in baskets on their backs supported by straps across their foreheads. Two years ago, this was a very prosperous place. It was the Depot for corundum that was mined twenty miles back in the hills and brought down here for deposit and transportation to the river. Since the close of the war, the company has closed down, and I doubt if they start again.

While corrugated iron for the roof of the permanent house was being brought from Calcutta and other building material was being sent from Jorhat, I had men working on two typical Indian mud houses, one of which I purposed to occupy during the approaching rainy season when building operations would be impossible. We staked off a space twenty-eight by fourteen feet, dug trenches around it where the eaves would carry the heavy rains, and threw the earth from the trenches back onto the house site, where it was levelled with pieces of wood and much walking over. Posts were put in the four corners and down the center for the ridge pole. Gangs of men went to the jungle to cut long reeds to use for laths for the walls, and bamboos for the frame-work of the roof, and for doors, beds, shelves, fences, etc. Thousands of bundles of tall thatch-grass were cut for the roof. The reeds were held in single straight rows by thin strips of green bamboo interlaced around every three or four reeds by two men, one on the outside of the house and the other inside, pushing the lacer in and out to each other. A similar bamboo lacer was used for tying thatch to the roof. The plaster was made by women mixing earth, cow-dung and water with their feet and smearing it over the reeds with their hands. The mud floor was smoothed and carpeted with layers of the same mixture made thin. Windows were holes cut in the walls. Outside, bamboo mats arranged to slide back and forth on bamboo poles, served as shutters.

There were two rooms fourteen feet square. One was entertainment-hall, dispensary, school-room, prayer-room, dining-room and storeroom. The center of the room was occupied by a pedestal extension table that my mother had donated to the new home. There were two large wardrobes, full of medical supplies, a folding organ, a magic lantern, a Victrola and records. Around three sides of the room bamboo bench tables, built with legs buried in the floor, held boxes of Bibles, hymnals, tracts, and Gospels printed in more than a dozen lan-guages. There were picture rolls, cases of soap, sewing supplies, and provisions stored in tin boxes that could not keep out the weavils. From ropes hung from the rafters, swung a screen box that protected the food from flies. The other room was a bedroom with a folding army cot, a bamboo bench for a dressing table and a big bamboo bed designed for six children.

One of the big purposes which from the very beginning, I had hoped my house might serve, was that it should be home for the half dozen little girls in Satribari that had come to us as babies, been legally adopted by the mission and knew no other life than that of the school cottages. I wanted my home to be the place where they might look forward to spending their vacations when the other girls go " home." The big bamboo bed was for these. Quite a number of our first boarding-school girls had married and were making little homes of their own in the villages around Hahim. I hoped that my presence in their midst might help them to incorporate into their own home life, some of the good things of home-making and mother-lore that they had learned at Satribari.

The night before I planned to move into this little cottage, I invited my neighbours in for a prayer service. I expected about a dozen or six-teen people, but thirty-two men, women and chil-dren came, besides about six babies tied to their mothers' backs. I was puzzled to know where to put my guests, but they solved the puzzle by re-ducing the pedestal table and bamboo shelves along the walls into uppers and lowers! One layer squatted underneath and another sat on the tables with bare legs dangling down. It was that hot part of the year before the rains break. There were three lanterns burning in the crowded room, but everybody was comfortable enough to stay for more than two hours.

During the months in which this little place was home there was not a day but that some one or some group squatted on my mud floor and heard of Jesus Christ. To many of them it was an en-tirely new story. At night mothers with their in-fants tied to their backs bent over books while their older children gamboled about unhampered by clothes, and when tired of play, curled up for a nap on the mud floor, with no more fuss than little kittens or pups, weary of play.

On a dark night, a line of blazing fagots traveled down the opposite hills, crossed the river and lighted the path to my house for two villages of fathers, mothers and children with the village teacher, come to see the magic something with which they had heard the white woman could make a great light without match, cinder, or other spark. So I exhibited my flash-light. Others came to see a doll that but few of the women and girls were daring enough to touch. Some were attracted by the bait of the Victrola, the organ, plow, the microscope, sewing lessons, medicines, and the peanuts planted in the garden. Though but few came just to hear of the things concerning Jesus, none left without hearing a word of this Saviour and Friend of mankind. Sometimes when the loneliness and isolation became well-nigh unbearable, it would have been easy to usher sufficient reasons to show the white feather and go back to the station. But close upon every acute attack of loneliness, God sent some message of His mindfulness and love, some service to render, some errand to run for Him. Parents brought sick children from back in the mountains, for medicine; a little fourteen-year-old zenana wife had to be helped through a hard siege of malaria and strengthened for the tax of motherhood; some needed help in their fight with opium; some of the Christians needed guidance along the way back to Christ.

One night I went to bed almost persuaded by the indifference of Christians and non-Christians, that my work was a failure. Early the next morning a Nepali woman was at the door saying that her husband was very ill. From all she said I gathered that the man must be suffering with cholera. Hastily packing into my Boston bag, Moore's *Family Medicine Book*, cholera tincture, and other things that I thought would be needed, and asking the Great Physician to supply the wisdom and skill I lacked, I hurried to the last bazaar hut, where the sick man suffered. The morning before he had been strong and robust, now he was emaciated as after a long, hard illness. It was undoubtedly cholera. We had no hot-water bottles, but heated stones and kept constantly massaging the man's cold arms and legs. Later collapse and hiccoughs set in, but we did not give up. At this stage Dr. Moore's book called for a mustard-plaster at the pit of the stomach. Having no mustard, I painted with iodine. That evening when bulbuls and Peking sparrows were singing vespers, I walked in the long shadows of great rubber trees, to my little hut, and my heart sang with the birds a song of praise for the beautiful world and all God's wonderful works, a song of gratitude that I had not run away, but had been on hand that morning when God needed someone to work with

Him to save, not only the Nepali cartman's life, but to prevent cholera from claiming the Nepali bazaar settlement where men, women and children lived sinfully in dark, crowded quarters.

When five of my old Satribari babies came to occupy my spare bed for the six weeks' summer vacation, there was no more loneliness, no further desire to play the coward and run away. With them about the place "Nengtakram" seemed a really-truly home.

Now for some more letters sent from far-off Assam to "the old folks at home":

April 21, 1922.

Dear Friends in Old "Second"*:

"Nengtakram!" I wonder if it sings for others as it does for me? It is the best Garo translation I can get for Rest Haven. A house and a garden all my own would be enough to make a singing in my heart, but this is more than a house and garden, —there is land enough to qualify for a little farm. . . . I got it from the Government for clearing the jungle off and paying for the first and second class trees on the place. I don't know how many big trees we cut down—enough to give us a fair view of the stars and the hills across the river, and there are still a number left for shade. I've left a big rubber tree in front of the site we have chosen for the bungalow.

* Second Baptist Church, Washington, D. C.

But there is more than land at Nengtakram. There is a stable with two cows, two calves, a pack-bull, and room for a pony when I get one. I am disappointed in my cows; they are supposed to be extra fine ones and to give two or three quarts of milk each, per day, but they scarcely give that much between them. . . . One of the little calves was born here on the place. She is the prettiest little thing; brown and silky and soft like a baby, and eyelashes so long that they must get all tangled up. I must have a pony for it is impossible to walk any considerable distance in this heat; then, too, there are so many rivers to cross and I could ford these most of the year on a pony. Sometimes there are men to carry me over pig-a-back or in a Queen's Chair, but oftener I wade and have been in water above my hips, and this doesn't pay.

For beasts of burden we have two water-buffaloes. . . . I have much fear and no admiration for these beasts, but they seem to be able to work in the hot weather with less discomfort than oxen. They spend most of the day in the water and work at night. You see, Nengtakram is forty-seven miles from Gauhati, so forty-seven miles from the railroad and white people. It is thirty-four miles from steamer-connection and tele-graph and ten miles from the post-office with no R. F. D. service, so I depend upon the buffalo cart to bring me provisions. For about six months of the year an auto can run between here and Gauhati, making the trip in three or four hours. But during the other six months the rains make most of the road impassable, so if I have to get out in these months, I'll have to go in the buffalo cart and spend three or four nights getting to Gauhati.

There is a weekly bazaar where I buy potatoes, onions, rice, chickens, and usually bananas of a kind. I haven't had eggs for more than a month, but have fixed a place for chickens so that the wild animals can't get at them. Now I can bring out my fowls and will be well off. . . . We had been living here but about two weeks when the bearer brought me a dead cobra one morning. He had been awakened about midnight by his chickens making a fuss. He keeps a few fowls for curry and they sleep under his bamboo bed. When he lit his tiny lamp and held it under the bed, there was this serpent! He slashed it several times with his native knife, so cut part of its hooded head off. I measured it with the surveyor's line and it stretched six foot and an inch from the tip of its tail to the piece of hood that was not cut off. I'm not going to let chickens sleep under my bed for I don't know what I would do if I found a cobra there.

In listing animals I mustn't forget my dog. . . . The place seemed mighty lonesome, especially at night, so I advertised in a Calcutta paper for a dog and in answer I have the nicest little mother dog with a three months' old puppy that isn't nearly as nice. The mother might have posed for the Victor trade mark, so like is she to " His Master's Voice." When I have to leave the place she stands guard near the fence, and it makes a tremendous difference coming back to have her bound out and say in every known dog dialect that she is so glad to see me. Just now the puppy is eclipsed by five of the little ones from Satribari. They have come to spend the six weeks' summer vacation with me and they make the place seem like home. They are aged from nine to four years. Most of them I took into Satribari when they were babies, so they seem like my really own folk. When they first came we had the nicest times working together in the garden in the early mornings and after sunset. Each child was the proud possessor of a little plot of her own, in which she planted seed in the morning and often uprooted them in the evening to see what had happened to them during the day. They go with me to the villages across the river to tell the wonderful story of Jesus and His love to those who understand Assamese. . . . They have been taking turns in sharing the general illness that is so prevalent here this year.

It hasn't been a good year for a novice like myself to begin farming for the usual storms that precede the annual rains have failed and there has been a great deal of heat. Twice the farmers planted their rice crops and the drought killed what

few sprouts came up. It has rained this morning
. . . and those who have seed will plant again, but
the grain should be three feet high now. I fear
some will be hungry before the next crop is har-
vested. And to think that there are streams all
over this section that might have watered the
parched ground. I planted some Country Gentleman corn twice, but the few blades that came up
burned. I am having more put out today. I
wanted to teach the people to plant peanuts, for
their diet is lacking in fats, and I think the nuts
will grow well there. I sent to Calcutta for two
pounds of the biggest, best peanuts to be had, for
planting. What came are tinier than we ever see
at home. But I planted them and gave some to
half-a-dozen others for their gardens and they are
doing better than anything else. In fact, out of
nearly four dollars worth of seed I have only several rows of peanuts and a few sick-looking canta-
loup plants. . . . I read a great, big book on
tropical gardening and thought that I was going to
help my farmer-friends here a whole lot. . . . As
it is, I find that instead of my teaching farming
to the people they are teaching it to me. And I
don't know but that this is the better way, for it
gives them a closer interest in the place and brings
them here oftener.

It is good, too, that there has been a delay in
building my bungalow, for scores of people come
to this little native house, so like their own, who

would be afraid to venture near a bungalow. You can't imagine how very primitive most of my friends and neighbours are. A simple little doll is so feared by girls in their teens, who are mothers, that they cannot be persuaded to touch it. But the young men hold it in the crook of their arm and kiss it! This might be just to appear brave before their women, for the male and female of the species are much the same, fundamentally, all the world over.

I love the nursing, especially of the children; and I love to have the women for Bible and sewing classes and to learn their letters, and I love to have them just come to sit with me at night, when I am not too busy. And I love to show them the wonders of the common things about us, as seen under my dandy little microscope. I'm more and more glad that I was extravagant and bought that microscope. The whole life is a wonderful mixture of sadness and gladness,—glad that you can help a little bit, and sad that it is such a little help where there is so great need. The two disheartening things that sometimes made me feel before the children came, that I couldn't stand it, but must run away, are the low moral tone of the Christians and the indifference and apathy that seem to settle upon my visitors when I begin to speak of spiritual things. It is at this juncture often, that some one yawns and suggests that they be moving on. In our little Hahim church last

week they expelled one man for stealing and another for drinking. I have learned since, that two
of those who sat in judgment upon these two and
had their names dropped from the church roll, are
not married although they have been living as man
and wife for more than two years and have a dear
little baby. Sad as this is, sadder is the fact that
the boy concerned is the teacher in the little school
here, and is the son of the village preacher and
Association evangelist, in whose house the couple
have been living these two years. And the girl is
one of my own Satribari girls whom I have been
holding up as a model Christian, never dreaming
that she was not married. The thing happened
while I was home taking care of Nettie. But I
suppose this very condition should make me glad
that I am here.

Last year I found this prayer of George Mathe-
son's, written, I judge, about the time he wrote,
" O, Love That Wilt Not Let Me Go," " Send me
to the hearts without a home, to the lives without
a love, to the crowds without a compass, to the
ranks without a refuge. Send me to the children
whom none have blessed, to the famished whom
none have fed, to the sick whom none have visited,
to the demoniacs whom none have calmed, to the
fallen whom none have lifted, to the lepers whom
none have touched, to the bereaved whom none
have comforted." I made this my prayer, too, and
Hahim Depot affords a fine opportunity for an-

swering it. But you must all pray for me. I fear
sometimes lest I may fail to put first things first.
Just now the biggest task I have on hand, apart
from trying to keep myself straight, is trying to
help little four-year-old Birsi control her sulky
temper. I have keen sympathy for her, remembering my temper was much the same as a child
and not so very different now. Birsi has made considerable advance.

Nengtakram, Hahim Depot,
16th June, 1922.

Dear Home-folk:

. . . School opened yesterday at Satribari and
I took the children in in ox-carts, going consider-
ably out of our way to attend several bazaars
where the children helped in evangelistic work with
their singing and reciting of Scripture. We left
here the sixth, traveled at night in carts, and in the
morning put up our organ at some weekly bazaar,
had a crowd in less time than it takes to write
about it, the crowd grew and pressed upon us until
I could scarcely breathe and couldn't see to read
the notes on the hymn book. They crowded from
behind until many times they almost upset the
organ. It was a little hard on the children, for
their food was not always regular, nor was it always good, and we were rather crowded for sleeping with seven of us and the dog in two little ox-
carts. . . . From six market centers we touched

hundreds of people who live a whole day's journey from these centers. There was some opposition in two places, but for the most we were graciously received and given a good hearing. These last two weeks I've felt more like a missionary than ever before.

The new Forest Officer thought that they might sell the jungakoli bungalow after all. Government is so deeply in debt, largely due to non-coöperation, that the Forest Department cannot keep up the road between here and Boko, which means that after a bit I will be ten miles from a road. Several bridges are already unusable even for ox-carts. Coming back from Boko yesterday morning we had to leave the road and take to the rice fields in one place because of a broken bridge, and this now before the heavy rains have commenced. . . .

In some ways I can't bear to think of leaving this place. I have my work nicely started and the people know me. Then there is the garden, but if the road is not kept up this will not be a good working base. . . . We are praying about it and have prayed about every step as we took it, so I know it will all come out right.

Jononi, the old Satribari girl who was engaged to be married and whose father had bought the provisions for the wedding feast when the boy broke off the engagement because Jononi was not very well, has been with me for some weeks now and is getting strong and well. I am very happy about this. I think it was indigestion and resultant weakness. I had her on a milk diet then gradually put her back on rice and she is gaining steadily. The boy who cast her off lost a jewel of a wife and the making of a beautiful mother. She was so wisely kind with the children when I had them here. She is one of the finest girls Satribari has produced,—not brilliant as a student, but generally fine and helpful. . . .

The perspiration is oozing from me; my hand sticks to the paper and my clothes are wet. The dolls sent out from home had heads made of some sort of composition stuff. The one I keep out showed signs of softening of the brain before I left on this trip and now its head has collapsed and fallen from the body. You would think that it had spent several days in water, but it has only absorbed the dampness in the atmosphere. My house is filthy from the work of insects and worms in the green wood. And oh, the bugs, the bugs! I want to cry about them, but instead I think I'll do some housecleaning. My poor dog has fever all the time nearly, and is peppered with prickly heat and insect bites. I'm going to begin today to give her quinine.

Those last ten days of the children's vacation spent jogging along in ox-carts at night and working in the bazaars during the day, were happy days

of seed-sowing for us all. We would hang our
Bible picture rolls on a tree, set up the organ and
begin to play hymns. Not even a musician could
have produced music from our worn-out little box.
But as soon as the first organ sounds fell on those
jungle bazaars, customers stopped buying and mer-
chants quit selling to join the crowd gathered
around the instrument. One would have thought
that Kriesler had come to town after having been
widely advertised. Men and boys climbed trees
for the advantage of box-seats from which to look
over the rest of the audience. Parents lifted small
children astraddle their shoulders that they might
see over the heads of the crowds. Throngs in front
swayed forward, tilting the organ with them; then
those in back surged close, jamming the children
and tilting the organ towards the front crowd.
Somewhere sandwiched between were the children
and I perspiring and asking for room to breathe
as I pumped out sounds that my audience accepted
for music. And they would remain to listen just
as long as I would consent to play, although nowhere in America have I been asked to play a second piece, for I know barely enough of notes to
play the treble cleff stumbling with both hands, an
octave apart.

The same thing was true of the medical work
I did. Every missionary in the jungle, dares in
those places of great need, what the laws of his

homeland wisely prohibit any other than a well
qualified medical person to attempt. When his
poor knowledge and skill is all that is available,
he dares not refuse to do his best for the needs that
are brought to him.

The great rains broke after I returned from taking the children back to Gauhati. Swollen streams
destroyed many of the bridges on the ten miles
separating us from the government cart road.
Continued rain buried much of the country under
water, made the river well-nigh impassable, spread
mould on shoes, and books and through the bread.
Insects ate the green bamboos with which the house
was built, showering on everything under the roof
a soft, tan powder, like flour, of which we would
dust and sweep away two or three quarts every
morning. The saturated atmosphere caused the
myriad seed of the earth floor to germinate, so
though I went to sleep at night with a perfectly
plain carpet of brown earth, I would awaken in the
morning to find it adorned with a design of
" green things growing." Mosquitoes multiplied
and seemed not to be discouraged by the thick
plaits of damp rice straw that we always kept
smouldering on the floor near our ankles at night.
Every crawling, creeping thing that had been hiding in the thatch came out boldly, now, to feast on
insects. One evening after killing nine enormous
spiders on the bamboo mats on the ceiling under

the thatch, we decided that it was a useless job
and left their fellows in peace. Almost everybody
dragged about with high temperature. Even my
little dog was peppered with bites where her coat
was thin, and it was pathetic to see her first shake
with chills then pant with fever.

VIII

TIMES OF STRESS

IN all probability I went back to Assam before
I was sufficiently recovered from the strain
of nursing Nettie, but those who knew me
agreed that I would probably be better for throw-
ing myself into my old work that so completely
engrossed me. Or it may be that because it did
so completely engross me, because I so loved doing
all the things that filled the days and nights, that
I failed to heed weariness and fever as I should
have. Much of the time since my return to Assam
I had suffered with malaria, more or less constantly,
but took quinine regularly, so seldom had a temperature over 103 and had spent but part of two
different days in bed. My heavy head of hair came
out until bald spots made it necessary to have my
head shaven. During the rainy season there was
no barber in the bazaar, but a community razor
was passed from house to house as needed, neighbours shaving one another. I called one of the
young farmers of the village, showed him how
easily a handful of hair fell from my head, and
predicted that the bald spots would grow until no
hair was left. Then I asked him to hunt the razor
and shave my head as sahibs shave their face. He

was rather unwilling to undertake the task, and expressed fear that after it was all shaven and could not be put back, the Missahib might regret and blame the barber in her mind.

When I had satisfied him that this would not be the case he went to hunt the razor while I prepared a kettle of hot water, soap, and a basin for suds. With the razor the barber brought a piece of stone (corundum) to use as a razor strop. He questioned the purpose of the hot water and soap and disdained its use after I explained that I had always used lather on my father's neck before shaving it. I think he put it down as due to the white man's inexplicable fondness for soap and water, and thought that it would be much easier to wash my scalp after it was shaven! Nevertheless, after he had cut away the long hair I hid the rest in a thick lather and he proceeded. He had worked about an hour, stopping several times to sharpen his razor on the rock, but produced little of the desired baldness. Suddenly I remembered a packet of safety razor blades my father had given me to use for ripping in sewing classes. I found these, but had nothing in which to hold the blade, so he held it in his thick fingers and reported better progress. The lather had long since disappeared; the water was no longer hot; my head felt like a series of ice-bound hills and the razor an ice-saw cutting away chunks.

The sun set. The bearer lit the lantern and

brought it in. After more than two hours' labour, the farmer-barber drew a long, deep breath and announced, " It is finished." Earlier in the day I had packed away my hand mirror, the only look-ing-glass in the establishment, but as I picked up the lantern to go into the bedroom, the strange, grotesque shadow of a head shaven and shorn fell on the mud wall and startled me so that I almost dropped the lantern, although it was a few seconds before I sensed the intimate connection between that shadowed head and mine. With gratitude, I remembered that during the four months in which the rains would keep me prisoner in the jungle, nature would do much towards repairing the dam-age done.

Constant rain made touring and most outside work impossible, and multiplied sickness and calls for medicine. These weeks in the house afforded the coveted opportunity for studying Garo. I wanted a facile use of this language for the win-ter's work in Garo villages.

When I had to go away for a short trip, there was a new baby in the cook's home, so I let him stay with his family and I started off in the buffalo cart with hard tack, canned fish and tea for the journey. Jononi was away. The last day of our return journey I was unable to get eggs, so had a can of fish for my eleven o'clock meal. I spent the heat of the day in the Government rest house and about four o'clock had a pot of tea before

starting our ten-mile ride to Hahim. The roads
were fairly washed away and so lost in muck
around broken bridges, that bullocks were not able
to pull carts through—all were dependent on buffaloes. Just before dusk, the old familiar aches
began to attack my joints and gnaw along the marrow of my bones. I curled up in the cart and
asked the driver to get home as soon as possible.
He did his best, but even buffaloes found it hard
to pull a cart through the mire of the worst places,
so it was after ten when we reached Nengtakram.
My coming was unexpected, and I found two of the
village girls sleeping nicely on the new hair mattress of my army cot. In short order they were
sent to their homes, but from fear of what they
probably left behind both from heads and bedding,
I had the canvas cot fixed for me.

That was a long, long night. Long before dawn
I knew that I was suffering from more than malaria
and wondered if it were cholera. The extreme heat
and the jostling of the ox-cart had probably hurt
the fish even though it did smell and taste all right.
In the early morning when the cook came in, I
was on the floor unable to get back in bed. His
sister-in-law, who understood and spoke nothing
but hill Garo, came in to help me. She was so
anxious to help but neither of us could understand
the other. I wanted a kimono from a tin trunk
of clean clothes. Muttering the magic word,
"Kee-mo-no," time after time, she roamed about

the house, lifting boxes, looking under and in them,
producing various articles of food, books, and
clothing, but nothing that resembled a kimono.
Finally the cook came in to assist. Then there
was a duet of murmured " Kee-mo-nos." I was
too weak and tired to talk much, but told the cook
that it was a big, light blue thing like a loose frock,
and had pictures of rice birds made on it in em-
broidery. Grasping desperately at the last of the
description, he hurried into the other room and returned with a hand-embroidered white tea-cloth!
" No, no, Boy; this isn't it! It is something I
wear over my gown when I get ready for bed at
night."

He changed his murmur to, " Something she
wears when she gets ready for bed at night," and
moved about in circles, a lost look on his perturbed
face. His sister-in-law jabbered with him in Garo,
beamed delighted intelligence, and hastened to get
the big, cane rod that she had seen me slip into a
noose to secure the door every night. If kimono
was connected with getting ready for bed at night,
surely this was it! I gave up the kimono quest
and called in the waiting village leaders for whom
I had sent.

They were anxious that some of my kind be with
me and wanted to send runners to bring aid from
Gauhati, or wanted me to go to Gauhati. I was
all but sure that I had cholera and knew that no
one could get to Gauhati and back with help in

time to be of service to me. In my condition such
a journey was impossible for me. Because in the
jungle death is swift, and in the rains, burial must
be within a few hours, I had told the cook that
I was to be wrapped in one of the bamboo mats
taken from the ceiling, and buried on the site
staked out for the house by the side of the road.
As soon as I had made my funeral arrangements,
I began to get better! Thanks to the emetine
which I found in the varied supply of medicines
with which clever Dr. Kirby had filled my emer-
gency case. Although I started the emetine in the
early morning as soon as someone came into the
house to get the case for me, it was night before I
could retain a tablespoon of water.

When I was able to sit in a chair, Hindu, Animist and Christian pooled their ingenuity and im-
provised a conveyance designed to get me over the
ten miles to the cart-road, for I could not have
stood that part of the journey in a cart. I had a
dining-room cane-bottomed chair with side arms.
Over these they tied high arches of lithe bamboo.
Over this framework they secured one long strip
of carpet-runner for hood and back, and two
shorter strips for side-curtains—the idea being to
afford protection from the heat of the sun and
the damage of almost certain downpours. These
carpet strips had laid by the side of my cot, in
front of the dresser and under my chair at the
table. My dog did not fancy mud floors and ap-

propriated the three pieces of carpet for beds on which she shed her white hairs. Vine thongs hung from the bamboo framework in which to put my arms to rest them. More thongs tied a small piece of wood to the lower part of the chair, for a foot-rest. When the chair was ready they had me sit in it to try it out while they adjusted the length of the arm and foot rests, to suit my comfort. A plaited strap came from ropes tied under the chair. This the carrier attached to his forehead and got into harness while stooping, then slowly rose to his feet with body bent forward, the chair resting on his back but most of its weight on his forehead.

The morning sun looked me in the face; my neck rebelled against the angle my head had to assume; my dog's white hairs and the dirt from the runner percolated down upon me. The carpet gave me the feeling of being smothered and I longed to dispose of the side-curtains, but feared to offend the friends who had so kindly provided them. As the day waxed warmer and we stopped to rest and change carriers, I had the side carpets taken down and went along in greater comfort. The relief coolie walked in front seeking the best footing, and several times when the carrier sank nearly to his knees in muck, the relief coolie helped him out with the stout stick that he carried. When on either side of the broken bridges, the six or eight inch cross-beam still spanned the stream the carrier walked over on this with his load rather than

try to ford the stream and be sucked in the mire
on either side. So sure-footed did I know these
jungle-men to be, that I was not nervous when carried in this fashion in the chair, eight to twelve
feet above a stream, on a single timber not wider
than the carrier's foot.

Just before noon we finished the ten-mile journey and I rested in the Government rest-house
until sunset, then started the night journey in a
hammock swung in the buffalo-cart that had been
sent on a day before. Just as we were leaving the
village, the Government mail-runner arrived and I
waited to see if there was anything for me in his
pack. They brought me a home parcel containing
a garden apron that my little mother had made,
and a blue gingham frock, chic and pretty with
elaborate cross-stitching on which Bertha had
worked warm summer evenings. Do you wonder
that with these two precious things fresh from the
loving hands of home folks hugged close, the night
in the buffalo-cart was not nearly so long as I had
expected it would be? The next afternoon Miss
Wilson brought her Ford out to the last rest-house,
and within an hour we made the remaining fourteen
miles of good road—a distance that the buffaloes
required all night to cover. Everybody in Gauhati
was so kind, doing everything possible to get me in
shape for the journey to the hills. Hearing the
sound of tinkling ice against a glass, I thought I
must be delirious, but opened my eyes to find Miss

Wilson by the bed with a glass of grape juice and crushed ice! She had sent a man across the river to meet the mail train and get the ice. When I was strong enough to make the journey, I went to dear Scotch friends in Darjeeling. The Himalayan cold brought out more malicious malaria, in treating which I took fifty-seven grains of quinine in twenty-six hours.

IX

WAYSIDE MINISTRIES

AFTER two months in the hills I returned to the plains looking and feeling remade, and eager to begin the dry season's work out in the district. While in Gauhati, I met our mission Executive Committee. With the Finance Committee, they had worked prayerfully, carefully and strenuously, trying to make appropriations cut twenty-five per cent, meet old needs as well as cover the expenses of new work, such as Miss Wilson's Home for Widows and Orphans, and my work in the district. Apart from my salary, I was allowed about three hundred dollars for the year's work; that is, for travel, pony, workers, tracts, supplies, etc. Even this amount had to be cut from other work, in addition to the twenty-five per cent cut on that work. This meant that I had to cut my expenses in one of two ways: either let Jononi go, or get rid of my pony. For many reasons it seemed impossible to do without my one Bible woman, especially since I lived and worked alone. Then, too, Jononi received but four dollars a month, whereas the pony stood me about seven dollars a month, so I decided to let the pony go, which meant that some days I walked thirteen miles,—

sometimes across rice fields and over hills. This little incident may help illustrate how deep a " cut " may go when applied on the field.

At this same session the Executive Committee requested that I work in the jungle but six months in the year and spend the rest of the time doing evangelistic work among the zenana or shut-in gentlewomen of Gauhati. Realizing that among other considerations the Executive Committee sought to save me the strain and wear of continuous work and residence in the jungle, did not lessen my intense disappointment over their action. From the first many of our missionaries questioned the expediency of a woman living alone so widely separated from colleagues, but I think none questioned the need of someone living in the midst of our Christian villages, where there was an apparent tendency to revert to non-Christian customs and standards. Being normal, I could not really relish the loneliness, but thought it not too great a price to pay until someone else should be sent to work with me, or better still, until a husband and wife should come and work the field together.

Failure to keep up the Hahim road and bridges made that place an impossible working base. We agreed that the permanent camp-house should be built at Boko, a village on the main cart road thirty-seven miles from Gauhati. Boko is the Government post-office for the surrounding country. All my Hahim mail was sent from and received

A FRIENDLY HINDU FAMILY OF GOOD CASTE

there. A great market gathers at Boko, Friday night and Saturday morning. It is the business center and rendezvous for Christians from more than a dozen villages. From Hahim we used to visit the market where we sold medicines, tracts, Gospels, played the organ and sang to gather crowds to listen to the Gospel. From the Government I secured an ideal piece of land along the river and on the road traveled by hundreds on bazaar days. Here I built a storeroom and gathered material for the permanent " house by the side of the road." While a coolie looked after the Boko material, I was able to rent a little two-room bungalow at Jungakoli, six-and-a-half miles back in the forest reserve. The place seemed designed to meet my very need. The house was built on a hill-top on posts twelve feet above the ground. I had the downstairs walled in and partitioned into a dining-room, little storeroom and large assembly-room, where the people gathered for Sunday school, Bible class, and entertainments. Fresh tints on the walls and oil on the woodwork made the place ready for my nice furniture, pretty draperies and good pictures. The finishing touch was a fence around a garden plot we tried to cultivate in front. All the time I occupied this bungalow, women came day after day to know if they might go upstairs and see the curtains, pictures, chairs, bed, looking-glass, etc.

Across the river sawyers had cut down great sal

trees—the only wood that white ants have any difficulty in reducing to powder. They cut the logs into required lengths which they rolled on to a trestle built in the hillside. One sawyer stood on top of the trestle and drew a big saw-blade up through the log; while the second sawyer stood below and drew the saw back. This was the primitive method used for sawing all the timber for the Boko camp-house, except the flooring, door and window-frames which were made by up-to-date machinery in our Mission Industrial School in Jorhat, and shipped to us. In spite of the crafty deception of the workmen, the delays in getting materials, and other disappointments, those months at Jungakoli were rich in happiness—happiness in the service of each day as it came and happiness in the years of service planned.

On Sundays, after Sunday school, a band of boys and girls went with me to visit non-Christian villages where we explained Bible pictures and the hymns we sang. We invited the people to the house and to the magic-lantern picture which we showed on a big sheet stretched between two trees at the foot of our hill. The lantern is a mighty evangelistic agency. Illiterate and educated Hindu and Mohammedan alike often refer to Christianity as the white man's religion,—a thing of the West symbolized largely by clothes (especially shoes, stockings and sun-hat). But let these objectors spend an hour or two squatting in the fields out

under the stars looking at pictures of a country of
hills and streams, of grain fields and palm-trees,
like those of their own countryside, and watch tur-
baned men and women in familiar flowing drapery,
move about in bare or sandaled feet, speak with the
very gestures of their own neighbourhood, use their
own familiar plow and yoke, their grass household
broom, open-lipped lamp, earthen vessels, and mill-
stone ground by two, and ever as they watch
the screen, they see in the midst of these picture-
folk that seem like neighbours, using their own
familiar things of the field and home, the Christ
of the Christians going about doing good. Ever
after they can think of Christ as belonging to them
in an intimate sense, as being more like themselves
than like the Europeans who preach about Him.
Then they are willing to believe that the Christ of
the Christians was born, not in the cold lands of
the north, to people of white skin, but that God
sent Him to a sunny south-land to a people of tan
skin. Non-Christians, who were not willing that
the Gospel be preached in their village, asked that
these pictures be shown there, that the women and
children might see them.

Some weeks the slides were shown in villages,
in bazaars, at Jungakoli, and out on the highway
where two roads meet, three or four nights. During the cold season the dew begins to fall heavily
right after sunset. Those in the audience who wore
shawls or blankets crouched in them as in a tent,

only their eyes peering through the open flap.
Even so, they got wet and chilled and I had to
swish the dew from the lantern table where it
trickled as though it had rained. Always after the
pictures and talk, I asked if there were any questions to be asked about the pictures or about Christianity? I would throw on the screen Hunt's picture of Christ, light in hand, knocking and waiting
outside a fast-closed door, and leave the picture
there while waiting for questions. One night in a
sal grove near Boko, when I asked if there were
any questions, a young Hindu farmer, a stranger
to schools and books, replied, " ' Questions'! If
you were to answer the questions that only I could
ask, you would be kept late. It is all so new and
strange, so different from anything that we ever
heard; how can we understand it when we have
heard but once? I have followed the lantern and
seen and heard three times, so I begin to understand a little. Missahib, I think if you stay here
long enough, and tell us often enough, we'll understand and may all become Christians." But there
are 27,000 villages just in Assam, so not many have
a chance to hear even three times.

Christmas Eve, 1922, I showed these Gospel pictures to a group of Hindu purdah women, most of
whom were Brahmins. We began with the Babe
born in the manger, followed Him through childhood to manhood, and His ministry in Galilee and
Judæa, the scenes of His popularity and of grow-

ing opposition to Him, His cruel trial and death, the empty tomb, His presence with His disciples as they walked by the way and in the Emmaus home and in our midst, outside every heart's door until it is opened, thereafter an ever-present Friend, " nearer indeed than breathing, closer than hands and feet." When I asked the women if they had understood the story and pictures, after some moments of quiet, a low-voiced young Brahmin widow said, " Missahib, I don't understand how they could treat Him so cruelly, when He was so kind and good? " For a second I had no answer, then I told my Hindu friend that I did not know how it could be, but that in all the years I had known Christ, He had been unfailingly kind and loving to me, yet, though I had not nailed Him to a tree, in other ways I had been ungrateful, as unworthy and as unkind to Him, as those in the picture were. I thought it must be because we do not think enough about Christ to grow like Him and so to be always kind and loving as He is.

X

CHRISTMAS ON A MISSION STATION

IN 1922 it was neither feasible nor possible to
have the Christmas tree at Hahim, as I had
planned. This was a keen disappointment
until I realized that God had wise and good reasons for overruling my plans and desires; that it
was not by accident that they had failed, nor had
God arbitrarily frustrated them. I had Christmas
in Gauhati, and it was a happy, busy time.

Christmas Eve I started off with a Sunday-school
picture-roll of the birth of Christ, and my hands
full of picture postals and tracts. Some of the
postals were those gay Christmas cards sewed together with coloured silk in long, blanket stitches,
in sets and in house shapes. As I went along the
road children saw the pictures and began to beg
for them. I told them that if they would come
with me to the Assamese carpenter's house they
would hear a beautiful story about the big picture
rolled up under my arm, and after I had told them
the story I would give them a picture. Quite a
number followed to the section where the carpenter lives. The Assamese carpenter is a Hindu, the
father of seven daughters and a son. The boy and
five of the girls have read in our school, so know

something of the Boy Who long ago in Joseph's carpenter-house " increased in wisdom and stature and in favour with God and man." Two of the girls are over thirteen years of age, so they have to remain indoors or in their father's court-yard until they are married. When I am in Gauhati, I have a little Sunday school in their house. From the dusty road, a step up of a foot or so brings one directly on to the tiny veranda, and thence into the " baita kana," or waiting-room, the public room beyond which men are usually not allowed. Four dusty, cobweb-laden pictures of Hindu gods and goddesses adorn the walls. I took down a picture of Krishna playing his flute and in its place hung the picture of the infant Christ in Mary's lap with wide-eyed cattle and adoring shepherds gazing upon Him. The carpenter's children know a number of our hymns, so we sang, " While Shepherds Watched Their Flocks," " He Has Come! The Christ of God," " Thou Didst Leave Thy Throne " and Luther's Cradle Song. Some of the other Hindu children standing about tried to sing with us. Then I told the glad, sweet story of Christ coming to earth as a weak little baby to bring peace to men and to tell them of God's love and good-will. For our memory verse we studied, " Unto you is born this day in the city of David, a Saviour, which is Christ the Lord." As he was able to repeat the verse perfectly, each child received one of the blanket-stitched cards. It was thrilling to see thirteen-year-old boys vie with eight-year-old girls to repeat the verse perfectly before the pack of special cards was exhausted. Thirty-two non-Christian children learned the text that morning.

Then I went to a Mohammedan section, stopped at the tailor's and hung the picture on a tree in his court-yard. None but the tailor's wife and two children would listen to the story. As they could not help with the singing, I sang only Luther's Cradle Song and passed on, meaning to go right to the bungalow. But on the way I saw twoscore or more men and boys playing football on the Police-Green. Some of the boys asked for pictures, so I hung the Christmas picture on a tree by the roadside and the men and boys stopped their game and listened to the story of the birth of the Son of God. Afterwards they, too, had pictures, and three or four cart-men passing by, jumped from their carts and asked for a picture with reading on it, and went off with Christian tracts.

In the afternoon some of the little girls from the boarding school went with me to tell the same wonderful story in song and speech to the wretched Deshwalli squatters who live by the entrance to Satribari. " Live," did I say? They stay there in grass shacks, laughing together in the morning, quarrelling in the afternoon, and making peace or continuing war at night. They sit, smoke, eat, and suffer with fever, right in the middle of the road.

Some of their children seem semi-imbecile and some are as bright and beautiful children as I have seen anywhere. The fact that they seem to miss nothing, that they are evidently unconscious of their abject wretchedness, shows how dormant or nearly dead their moral sense is. At first I could hardly endure trying to tell them of Christ—they were so heedless and rude that I felt helpless. Then I remembered that the message I have is the " power of God unto salvation " and can cause even such as these to " arise from the dead."

Before dinner that night the Satribari girls came to the bungalow to sing Christmas carols and receive the gifts which were distributed from the boxes sent out from America. What dandy, generous boxes they were! . . .

After dinner the magic-lantern was taken to a school which the Mission runs for high caste children in a section of the town where Assamese gentlefolk live. Here we showed slides on the life of Christ to Hindu purdah women. What a contrast the quiet attention of these women furnished to the afternoon audience of Deshwalli squatters! After finishing describing the slides, I asked if there were any questions,—if the pictures had been understood. After a moment's quiet, a gentle-voiced woman said, " The last of the pictures were so sad! How could they be so cruel to one so kind and good? " Then I knew that the pictures had told their story well.

Monday morning at Chota (early breakfast) we found generously filled stockings over the backs of our chairs and had fun unwrapping our gifts. There was a morning service on the old compound, followed by sports and tea on the lawn. I ran away from the sports to visit in the homes of the neighbourhood to invite the women and children to a magic-lantern talk in the church that night just after dark. Women came from only one household, but some forty children sat on the front benches and watched with eager eyes and remarks as the life of Christ was pictured for them.

Christmas Day closed with dinner and a happy social evening. Maybe you are as keen as my mother to know what we had to eat? Fruit cocktail, soup, roast goose, dressing, baked corn, salad, a tart red jelly something like cranberry sauce, mince pie, plum-pudding with butter sauce, candy, almonds, and coffee. Now was it not foolish of my little mother to grieve on such occasions because she thought I had nothing good to eat? As we said " good-night " to our host and hostess, some of us tiptoed to the side of the bed where baby Margaret slept, and we marveled anew at the wisdom of God in sending the world's Saviour to earth as a helpless Babe needing a woman's loving care.

No! it was not the Christmas I had planned, but who could ask for a richer, more blessed two days?

XI

LAST DAYS IN ASSAM: ORDERED HOME

AFTER Christmas one of my dear Scotch friends went with me to Jungakoli for a two weeks' Bible class for former Satribari students and a week's tour of bazaar centers. As most of our old girls had babies and household duties that prevented them from leaving home, only six were able to spend the two weeks in Bible study. Some of the girls brought questions that showed they had been thinking and studying since leaving school. Classes were held from nine to eleven, and two to four. We had Bible drill in locating and quoting favourite passages, worked out an outline of the prophets, studied some of the women of the Bible, and translated Andrew Murray's *Working for God*. Sunami was one of the original eight girls sent to Satribari by the women of the Christian Association. After finishing her school-work she returned to her village and was married to a young man who had been appointed as teacher-pastor in a non-Christian village where several had accepted the Christian faith. Sunami had a little girl about eighteen months old at the time of the Bible class. While studying the prayer Christ gave us, Sunami asked, " Missahib, do you think it means that you must forgive everything, no matter what it is? "

181

" Yes, I think it means just that, Sunami, if we expect Christ to forgive us everything, no matter what it is. ' Forgive us our debts, *as* we forgive our debtors.' "

" Oh, but Missahib, it is so hard sometimes to forgive *everything* like that!"

" Yes, Sunami," I said, " it is one of the hardest tasks to which Christ calls us." A sober earnestness in Sunami's face and voice made me remember her question.

Imogini, one of the girls attending the Bible class, had suffered with ingrowing eyelashes from childhood. Twice while she was at Satribari, we operated on her eyelashes, but the trouble recurred and for a year Imogini had sat in a corner of the house able to see only a shaft of light and expecting that this, too, would soon be swallowed up in darkness. After two weeks' pleading the girl's father consented to her going to Calcutta to see if anything could be done to help her. The last night that she was with us, I took the blind girl for a walk. Seeing tears roll down her cheeks, I supposed Imogini was fearful of what might await her in Calcutta, so began to speak comfortingly to her. " No, no, Missahib! I am not crying because of what might be; that is not in my mind. I am thinking how good God is! For a year I sat in the house and never hoped to go about again. I did not even go to church. Now I have already journeyed across three rivers to come here. I am visiting, hearing the voice of friends, and learning about the Bible, and I am to go to Calcutta. I thought God had forgotten me and just see what good things He has done for me! I'm crying because I am happy. I know now that God was planning these good things for me all the time I supposed He had forgotten all about me!"

Imogini's sight could not be restored, but she was admitted to a Calcutta school for the blind and is living happily with other sightless girls and women learning Braile, basketry and knitting, so that when she returns to her village she need no longer sit useless in a corner.

Up to this time most of my touring had been in non-Christian villages. Until building the camp-house at Boko should keep me in that place I purposed to spend most of the time making six-day visits to our Christian villages. Usually I was quartered in the schoolhouse or church. The day began with morning prayers with the women and children, for I coveted for all of our Christians the strength and joy of family prayers in each home, and hoped to help the women to have this. After early breakfast I visited in the homes, calling at every house in the village. In the afternoon the women came to sew. Most of them were very clever at weaving, but few of them knew anything about needlework; and how eager they were to learn and how loath to put the needle away when the sun drew close to the western hills and they had to go home to prepare the evening rice, while Jononi and I sought out those in the village who no longer walked in the Christian way but were under church discipline.

In all these interviews with offending and offended Christians, I realized anew how like our human nature is in spite of the differences in the colour and customs of the races. Jononi's father had not been to church for more than a year. He said that he had been falsely accused and placed under church discipline. He was offended and hurt, so would not attend any of the church services. Then when his fellow Christians seemed not to notice his absence and failed to remonstrate with him for it, his feelings became more and more hurt and he said that they did not run after him because he was poor and ignorant! We persuaded him to attend services the next Sunday, and he found many calloused brown hands seek his in greeting and gladness that brown tongues find difficulty in phrasing.

In Santipur we called on a man who had taken to drink and had not been to church for two years. He had just returned from his work in the fields, weary, dusty, and hungry. As he squatted under the eaves of his cottage while Jononi and I stood in the courtyard, he looked me straight in the eyes and began this story: " Yes, Missahib, I have not been to church for two dry seasons, and," bowing his head and speaking low, faltering words, " I drink with the heathen. It was like this: we had been long married and had no children. Then this boy came, and oh, Missahib, he was a wonderful boy! Then he had hard fever, very hard. We went to the jungle and got all the roots and leaves that are good for fever but it did no good. He got hotter and hotter and died. When he died they were drinking in that heathen village across the river. I went over and drank with them until I forgot all about it. And ever since, when they make rice beer over there, I go over and drink until I forget again."

"Are you happy drinking rice-beer and forgetting about a wonderful boy God gave you?" I asked the man.

A big, dusty hand wiped tears from a face lined with suffering.

"God knows, I am not happy! But, Missahib, God cannot be the kind of God you say He is. Why did He let my boy die?"

"That I do not know," I replied, "but I do know that God's love may be safely trusted in life and death. How can we who are familiar with only this little courtyard of life, know the why of God's inviting our children, who are also His children, into the life of His Home? All of love that we know we have learned of Him; surely we may trust our dear ones to Him Who is also their Father and Who uses the terms of parenthood to

help us understand the tenderness of His love and
of His desire for our welfare? "

Just then I noticed a baby creeping about the
courtyard and asked whose child it was. Almost
casually the man answered, " Oh, that is mine.
But he is just like all the children in the village; he
is not the wonderful boy the other was."

" Don't you think that if you give up drink and
go back to the Christian way—if you become to
this little one the good father you were to your
other son,—don't you think that maybe God will
help this baby become the same wonderful sort of
child your other son was? "

And the bereaved man cried, " Oh, Missahib,
I'd like to try it!"

And there in the courtyard where the ordinary
baby was playing about, we thanked our Father
that in His wisdom and love He has seen fit to set
us in families and let us know the joy and blessing
of little ones in our homes. And we thanked Him
for His Father-love and patience that encourages
us to get up from a tumble and reach out for His
strong, steadying hand while trying to learn to walk
and find our way Home.

The next prayer-meeting night this man walked
again along the neglected path to the little church-
school and standing in front of his neighbours, said,
" You all know what kind of a man I have been
these last months, so I do not need tell you that.
But you do not know what an unhappy man I have

been. I want to come back and try again, if you will give me another chance." The other chance was given, and the man made good.

In Sunami's village I learned that just previous to the Bible class Sunami's husband had been expelled from the school he taught, because of love letters sent and improper advances made to one of the girls in his school. While he was teaching school, Sunami had done considerable work on their cultivation. The sun had put streaks of straw colour through the black strands of her hair; wind and sun had roughened her skin; the hoe had calloused her hands; and she looked fagged and weary. Her husband complained to her that she was not good enough for him, that she did not please him as the younger girl did. Then I remembered the pointed question about forgiveness that Sunami had asked in Bible class. The people in her village said that not once had they heard her reply to her husband's taunts. As we talked of her problem, this girl out of the tragic experiences of her young life taught her old teacher a lesson on love, " Missahib," she said, " I know now, why God makes us forgive like that. It is because He wants us to be happy and we can't be happy if we do not forgive. I know if I live a true Christian life that my husband will become a Christian again and love me." A letter I received from Sunami, reports that her husband is back in the church, superintendent of the Sunday school, and all is again well with my girl.

On Sundays some of the men and older boys would accompany me to neighbouring non-Christian villages where we sang and talked of Jesus. On these trips the men did most of the talking. Their method of approach was usually something like this:

"No; we are not working in our fields today, because we are Christians and give one day in the week to serving the Lord who sends sun and rain to make our rice grow. We used to be just like you—did all the things you do and were afraid of all the things you are afraid of. Why, at night we wouldn't pass that bamboo clump at the fork of the fields, where you say that evil spirits live. We didn't like to pass it alone during the day either, and no one could have paid us to cut a bamboo from it. But now that we are Christians, we do not believe in evil spirits, so we cut bamboos from this clump just as freely as from any other clump. It is the same way with all the rocks we used to fear as places where evil spirits stay. It is very good not to be afraid of trees and rocks.

"How many people in this village can write their name or read the wrapper around a bottle of quinine tablets? Not one! That's just the way it used to be in our village before we were Christians! But in most Christian villages many boys and girls go to school and can write letters and read books through. They can read for themselves a Book God wrote for us—for you and for us—and it is the things written in His Book that make us so different from what we used to be, that we are like new people. And these are the things we have come to tell you about."

So often the older people responded to the message by saying, " Tell these things to young people, but we are too old to change our thoughts or customs or lives. We have lived as Hindus, and as Hindus we will die."

Before finishing the tour of the Christian villages I accidentally discovered that I had lost the hearing of my right ear, so went to Calcutta to see a specialist, hoping to return to Assam after a fortnight and begin to build the Boko house. In order to secure the ear specialist's services, I had to enter the Presidency General Hospital and was put in the ward where I had visited Nettie, my bed looking out on the veranda bed she used to occupy. After the first examination, the surgeon told me that I ought not to live in Assam or any other damp place. Remembering the house to be built " by the side of the road," I hardly considered his opinion. Before the second examination I had an attack of fever and was amused to have ice-packs put at my head, my temperature taken every hour, and the nurses told to keep me quietly in bed, for I had marched in the jungle with as high temperature, and of course never had ice. But it seemed a more serious matter after the next interview with the surgeon in

which he said that under no circumstances should
I return to the jungle, but that I ought to return
to the United States and live in some dry, non-
malarial section. When I suggested that he take
care of my ear and ignore the malaria, he assured
me that the two were closely connected, that the
malaria was of the malicious type and had been too
long ignored. He predicted that if I returned to
work in the jungle, that certainly before two
months I would have to be carried out.

I had come to consider that all the previous
years of my life had been in preparation for the
service of the " house by the side of the road," so
these physical developments seemed a nightmare
from which I must shortly waken. Just when car-
penters were to have commenced work on the permanent house at Boko, I went to dismantle the
Jungakoli bungalow, pack my belongings, dispose
of the cattle, and bid my old friends farewell.
There was a woman at Boko named Satmi, whom
I particularly hated to leave. I found Satmi in a
village of opium-eating Garo squatters. When I
asked her if she had ever heard of Jesus Christ, she
amazed me by replying that she was a Christian.

" You a Christian and in this village of opium
eaters! How does that happen? " I asked.

" It was this way, Missahib," said Satmi.
" When I was a child I lived up in Kotiatoli,
in Nowgong district, and Mr. Moore baptised me.
Then I married one of the boys of that place and

afterwards he ran away with someone else. Then so many of the people were sick with Kalaazhar and so many had died of it, that the rest of them went away to different villages wherever they could find a place to stay. My mother and father died and I ran away and stayed in the village of the man in whose house I am now. Cultivation in that village was poor, so we moved around and finally came here. Everybody here eats opium. My husband ate it and then I did."

"Satmi, do you remember anything about Jesus?"

"I remember that we used to have a church-building where we went Sundays," the woman answered, "and some other times, and that we used to pray, but I cannot remember what we prayed. And we used to sing songs that were different from the songs that the heathen sing, but I cannot remember these, either."

"Would you like to give up opium, Satmi?"

"Oh, Missahib, who that eats it would not like to give it up!" So we knelt in front of her eight-by-ten hut and asked God to enable Satmi to do this very difficult thing. Then I went back to camp.

The next morning I sought out Satmi and asked her if she had taken opium since I had seen her.

Looking in my face she replied without stammer or hesitation, "Yes, Missahib. Did you see that man by the side of the house when you went? Well, as soon as you left, he offered me some. Now wouldn't it have been a pity not to have taken it when I could get it for nothing? "

" Satmi, if I had been here would you have taken it? "

A slight shadow of trouble rested on her face as Satmi answered with deliberation, " No, Missahib; I think not; because you wouldn't have liked it."

" You are right, Satmi, I wouldn't have liked it. But Satmi, I never saw you before yesterday, never knew anything about you; I never even heard of you before.   It is because Christ cares about your taking opium, oh, so much more than I could, that I care. He does more than care. He can help you, but I cannot. In a few minutes I'll have to go away again, but He never has to leave you. And, Satmi, you can talk to Him at any time; you do not even have to move your lips to do it, and He will close your fist so tightly that no one can force opium into it."   Again we knelt to ask the ever-present Saviour to help Satmi win her battle.

The next morning when I sought Satmi out, she reported victory, and also the day following. The fourth day she said, " No, Missahib, I haven't had opium, but I am sick."   So I gave her medicine for the disorder that troubles anyone breaking with a drug habit.

About six weeks later I was again on tour in Satmi's neighbourhood, and sought her out. Be-

fore she could report, an old man of the village
came to me and said, " Missahib, give me some of
that medicine like you gave Satmi. She has quit
opium, and I want to give it up, too."

Satmi interposed excitedly, " Medicine does not
make you give up opium. I trusted God and He
helped me give it up. Then when I had given it
up, I got sick. And when I got sick, the Missahib
gave me medicine! Now if you want to give up
opium, you'll have to trust God and He will help
you give it up. Then you will get sick. And then
the Missahib will give you medicine!"

Before making my farewell visit to Satmi, I
asked God for a message for her—something that
could stay by and help her after I had been forgotten. And I looked through that rich old storehouse of truth, but found nothing that satisfied me.
All the way along the narrow trail through the
jungle grass, I sought for a message, but none
came. Satmi brushed a clean place in front of her
straw shack and placed her inverted rice-pounder
for a seat for me. In the gully by Satmi's house
the first rains had brought out the early pink lilies,
in the parched grass of the long dry season. This
stubble mixed with cow dung was fashioned into
thin flat cakes which were dried in the sun and
used for fuel. These with a shadow of wings on
the courtyard and the " caw, caw," of the crows,
gave me Satmi's message.

" Satmi, Satmi, come here and look at the crows; for they neither sow nor reap; which neither have storehouse nor barn: and God feedeth them: How much more are you better than the fowls? And Satmi, look at the lilies how they grow: they toil not, they spin not; and yet I tell you truly, that the Raja in all his durbar-glory was not arrayed like one of these. If then, God so clothe the grass, which is today in the field, and tomorrow is cast into the oven, how much more will He provide for you? "

Over and over again I repeated the verses, then asked Satmi to say them back to me.

Then I said, " Satmi, after I have gone, I want you to say these words to the other women and children here in the village. And if anyone ever tells you that God doesn't care about you and that it doesn't make any difference to Him what happens to Satmi, then I want you to say these verses to yourself. That is why I want to be sure that you have them."

Shaking her head, Satmi replied, " Missahib, I've never been to school, how can I say all those words like you said them? But I can say them this way: When I see the flowers and hear the birds I'll say, ' Satmi, the birds say, and the flowers say, God thinks about us, and looks after us. You are much bigger than we are, Satmi, so He thinks about you, too, and will take care of you.' "

This is just a little glimpse of the grain ripened in one small corner of the great field. Was the little lone reaper taken from the field and from active service in order to give this report, and to show that even the least-skilled and the most unworthy, may go at the bidding of the Lord of the harvest and with the sickle of love help to gather in the sheaves?

THE END

Books on CHINESE LIFE

The Gateway to China
By Mary Ninde Gamewell
Pictures of Shanghai Yesterday and To-day.
A new, revised edition. Mrs. Gamewell has contrived to catch and hold China's colorful panorama, and furnish a diverting and informative description of its origin, manners, customs, people, politics and enterprises. Illustrated, $2.00.

New Lanterns in Old China
By Theodora Marshall Inglis
Stories of Chinese life by the wife of Dr. John Inglis, who was for some years in charge of the Au Ting Hospital, China. Based on personal experiences they visualize with rare fidelity the sights and scenes of everyday life in the Orient.
Illustrated, $1.25.

The Chinese Boy and Girl
Illustrated, $1.75. By Isaac Taylor Headland

Chinese Mother Goose Rhymes
By Isaac Taylor Headland
"Since Dr. Arthur H. Smith's popular books on the Chinese people, nothing of greater interest on China has been written than Prof. Headland's."
—*The Congregationalist.*
Illustrated by the author, $1.75.

China the Mysterious and Marvelous
By Victor Murdock
"All the more instructive for being so astonishingly entertaining."—*Review of Reviews.*
Illustrated, $2.50.

China from Within
By Charles Ernest Scott, M.A.
Introduction by J. Ross Stevenson, D.D. "A striking and engrossing account of the inner life of China."—*Missionary Review of the World.*
Illustrated, $2.00.

OTHER BOOKS ON CHINA

The Chinese as They Are
$1.50. By J. R. Saunders, Th.D.

Chinese Heart Throbs
$1.50. By Jennie V. Hughes, M.D.

Village Life in China
Illustrated, $2.50. By Arthur H. Smith

Chinese Characteristics
Illustrated, $2.50. By Arthur H. Smith

The Education of Women in China
Illustrated, $1.50. By Margaret E. Burton

Notable Women of Modern China
Illustrated, $1.50. By Margaret E. Burton

The Foreign Relations of China
$4.00. By Mingchien Joshua Bau, M.A., Ph.D.

TRAVEL AND DISCOVERY

JAMES BAIKIE, F.R.A.S.

Author of "Wonder Tales of the Ancient World,"
"The Story of the Pharaohs," etc.

A Century of Excavation in the Land of the Pharaohs

32 full page illustrations. $3.00

"This new account of excavations in the Nile Valley, beginning with the pioneers and bringing the story up to 'Tutankhamen and his splendors' is sure of both welcome and appreciation. A masterly survey of the whole field, furnished by a scholar in complete mastery of his subject and in full command of its material."—*Boston Transcript.*

D. E. LORENZ, Ph.D.

The 'Round the World Traveller

With 8 maps, 60 illustrations, etc. $5.00

"The author is a director of round-the-world cruises, and he has himself made the trip many times; he knows what the ordinary traveler most wishes to be told. The volume not only offers valuable service to the tourist, but the stay-at-home reader will find that its survey of essential facts and important points of interest make a handy reference book."—*N. Y. Times Book Review.*

W. D. WESTERVELT

Author of "The Legends of Old Honolulu"

Hawaiian Historical Legends

Illustrated. $1.50

"Covers almost every phase of Hawaiian and Polynesian life—manners, customs, religious beliefs, together with the records of deeds of daring done by voyagers and warriors. A volume of exceptional interest, not only so far as its story element goes, but as a veritable storehouse of Hawaiian information."—*Rocky Mountain News.*

SOCIOLOGICAL

ROGER W. BABSON

Recent Labor Progress

With Special Reference to the Work of the Federal Government under James J. Davis, Secretary of Labor. $2.00

An informed, authentic, sympathetic study of the powerful and broadening influences which have been moulding the Federal labor policies in recent years, related by a man whose name is that of the best known economist of his time, including:

Story of Secretary Davis' Life	Trade Union Progress
Immigration	Educational Charters
Workmen's Compensation	Employment
Woman in Industry	Standards of Living
Profit-Sharing Plans	Child Welfare
Conciliation	The Wage System
Naturalization	Religion
Old Age Insurance	